The Sommers Scandal
The Felling of Trees and Tree Lords

Betty O'Keefe and Ian Macdonald

Heritage House

CANADIAN CATALOGUING IN PUBLICATION DATA

O'Keefe, Betty, 1930-
  The Sommers scandal

Includes index
ISBN 1-895811-96-1

1. Sommers, Robert, 1911-
2. British Columbia—Politics and government—1952-1972.*
3. Foresters—British Columbia—Biography.
4. Businessmen—British Columbia—Biography.
5. Forest policy—British Columbia—History.
I. Macdonald, Ian, 1928-
II. Title.

FC3827.1.S66033 1999   971.1'04'092   C99-910744-5
F1088.033 1999

First edition 1999

Heritage House wishes to acknowledge the financial support of the Government of Canada and Heritage Canada through the Book Publishing Industry Development Program, and of the British Columbia Arts Council. Thanks also to the staff of the British Columbia Archives and Records Service (BCARS).

Cover and book design by Darlene Nickull
Edited by Audrey McClellan

HERITAGE HOUSE PUBLISHING COMPANY LTD.
Unit #108 - 17655 66 A Ave., Surrey, BC V3S 2A7

Printed in Canada

Canada

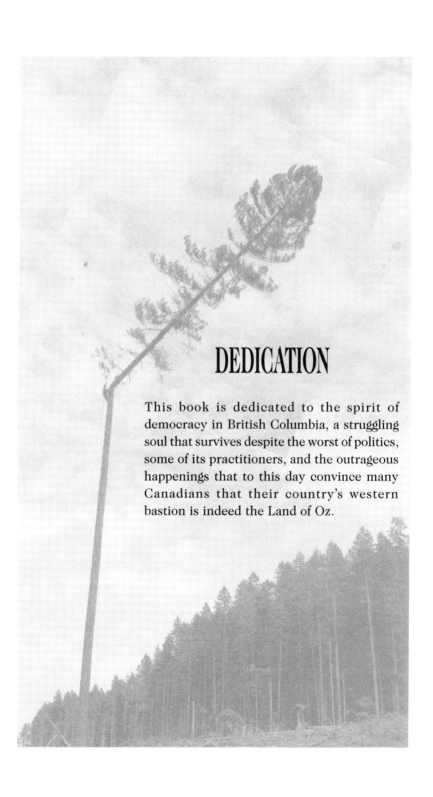

DEDICATION

This book is dedicated to the spirit of democracy in British Columbia, a struggling soul that survives despite the worst of politics, some of its practitioners, and the outrageous happenings that to this day convince many Canadians that their country's western bastion is indeed the Land of Oz.

CONTENTS

Robert Sommers was born in 1911 in Alberta, but moved to British Columbia where he completed his education. He became a schoolteacher and primary school principal in the Interior town of Castlegar. In addition to his teaching duties, Sommers was a trumpet player and leader of a band that travelled through the Kootenays, performing at various social functions and fund-raisers. He also sold insurance during the summer months and was a volunteer firefighter.

PROLOGUE

The Tea Party

In the elegant living room of the plush Toronto mansion, they sat delicately balancing teacups and talking trees. It was the fall of 1954. The host, Edward Plunkett "E.P." Taylor, multimillionaire industrialist, financier, sportsman, and racehorse owner, wanted more trees for his expanding West Coast company. And what E.P. wanted, E.P. usually got.

New to such surroundings was Robert E. Sommers, until two years earlier a small-town school principal and part-time trumpet player, insurance salesman, and forest firefighter. Now, however, he was in a position to recommend whether or not E.P. got what he wanted.

A man of many parts, Bob Sommers had hit new heights when he ran for elected office in the 1952 British Columbia provincial election. Since August of that year he had been the Honourable Robert E. Sommers, rookie politician and all-important minister of lands, mines, and forests in the brand-new Social Credit government. He was well aware that only his ministerial position put him face to face with E.P. Taylor and some of the high-ranking executives gathered at the Taylor estate in Toronto.

The get-together had been arranged because Sommers was in the east to attend his daughter's wedding, and E.P. wanted to discuss some difficulties encountered by his relatively new B.C.-based company, British Columbia Forest Products (BCFP).

About seven years earlier, H.R. MacMillan, owner of the highly successful forest exporting company that bore his name, convinced Taylor he should get into the B.C. forest industry. At this time, Taylor's Argus Corporation was one of Canada's largest conglomerates. On MacMillan's advice, Argus purchased several B.C. logging and milling operations for $4.5 million and incorporated BCFP, which initially produced only logs and lumber. Anxious to expand into pulp and paper

After serving as a "dollar-a-year man" in Ottawa during the Second World War, Edward Plunkett "E.P." Taylor became a titan of Canadian industry in the post-war years, establishing the mighty Argus Corporation, headquartered in Toronto. Taylor was a multi-millionaire, a leader in the financial community and in society, a sportsman and owner of winning racehorses. Argus's westward expansion included a B.C. forest company that needed more trees to make it a bigger player on the West Coast. A powerbroker, what E.P. wanted, E.P. usually got. His ambition for his company triggered the Sommers scandal.

production, Taylor backed BCFP's 1948 application for one of the newly introduced Forest Management Licences (FMLs), but the request was turned down. E.P. didn't know why.

In fact, the provincial forest service was suspicious of the profit-hungry Eastern corporation, fearing Argus would have little regard for the future of B.C.'s forests and might just "cut and run," taking what profit it could get immediately and leaving B.C. with land stripped of its natural worth.

When BCFP applied for its licence, the province had just implemented a new forest management system based on recommendations in the 1948 report of a royal commission on forest practices. The Commission had been set up a few years earlier to investigate public fears and criticism that the freewheeling tree cutting, common since the arrival of the first settlers a century earlier, was beginning to devastate parts of the provincial forest. The area of concern included much of southwestern B.C. and Vancouver Island, where the province's prime stands of Douglas fir were located and where much of the forest industry was centred.

Until this time, little thought had been given to regeneration of the forests, as it was believed "mother nature" would take care of herself. By the 1940s, however, there were suspicions nature was having trouble, and the forest service took on the role of encouraging more reforestation as well as tightening up enforcement of regulations. Under the FML system, which was introduced in 1948, large companies were given cutting rights to substantial areas of provincially held Crown land in perpetuity. In exchange, licence holders had responsibilities to manage the forest carefully, to ensure new trees were planted when they didn't regenerate naturally, to prevent and control forest fires, and to provide good access roads for logging trucks and firefighting equipment. The goal was to create a sustained yield for the forest industry, ensuring a new tree grew for each one felled, thereby guaranteeing trees for the future. The forest management areas were to be large enough to supply mills on a continuing basis, and different areas within the FML would be harvested each year in rotation. The forest service recognized it could not manage the whole forest on its own, but it could liaise with the large companies to ensure the job was being done properly.

It was Robert Sommers' responsibility to encourage or reject new FML applications from the larger companies. On his recommendation, applications were passed to the forest service for assessment, adjustment, and approval. Applications accepted by ministry personnel were then returned to Sommers, who presented them to his cabinet colleagues for final approval. Sommers controlled a process that brought more money into the province and provided more jobs and more taxes for provincial coffers than any other. Enterprises could rise or fall on his recommendations, and millions of dollars in the value of a company's shares were at stake each time a licence was approved or rejected.

The FML system that had developed by 1954 had one great, glaring weakness. The Social Credit government, like the Coalition government before it, had not spelled out the criteria by which the minister accepted or rejected the initial applications, only the criteria for the forest service approval process. The door was left open for manipulation; special deals could be arranged for old friends, party coffers filled when the need arose, and under-the-table arrangements accommodated. The system could be used for political payoffs and bribery—partisanship at its worst.

Sommers listened as Taylor and his directors made their case for ambitious expansion in B.C. He heard about their frustration and their disbelief that their intentions had been misunderstood by the forest service in their first application. Sommers received a polished message from the men at the top of Argus Corporation.

It was some four years after the door swung open at Taylor's mansion that another door clanged shut for Robert Sommers in the grey-walled grimness of the B.C. Penitentiary in New Westminster. The "tea party" had a direct effect on what happened in the intervening years and what eventually became of Robert Sommers after the longest trial in the province's history to that time.

The Sommers case triggered the gravest political crisis in the twenty-year reign of Premier W.A.C. Bennett, leaving a great blot on the picture of political purity he painted during his first election campaign. When Bennett took over, he was adamant that there would be no patronage appointments, no special deals, no payoffs to old friends for favours. He believed this was one of the factors that had killed the previous Coalition government, and he insisted his "unassuming little group" would take the moral high ground. But money did change hands, Bob Sommers went to jail, E.P. Taylor got his sought-after licence, and to this day many wonder at the confusing array of verdicts brought down in the Sommers case.

THE SOCREDS

If any bets were taken on B.C.'s 1952 provincial election, the odds would have been in favour of a first-time win for the CCF. The right-wing vote was split three ways between the Liberals, the Conservatives, and a new group calling itself the Social Credit Party. The outcome of that vote was to shape the province's future for the next twenty years.

Out With the Old

The people of British Columbia wanted a change in the legislature when they went to the polls in 1952, and they got perhaps more than they bargained for. Their new government was a rookie line-up of eighteen men and one woman representing an almost unknown political party. Only two, the man who would be premier, William Andrew Cecil Bennett, and the woman, Tilly Jean Rolston, had any experience in the provincial House. They had previously crossed the floor to sit in the legislature as independent members, having abandoned their old Conservative-Liberal Coalition loyalties. Bennett had abandoned the Coalition twice, once to try unsuccessfully for a federal Tory seat because he found the provincial government ineffective, and once when he returned to provincial politics but again found himself at odds with the premier, Byron Johnson. He soon persuaded Rolston to join him, first as an Independent and then as a member of a new party.

The new Social Credit (Socred) members of the legislature flocked to Victoria, still excited and amazed at their victory and the large representation they had achieved. They were caught up in the wonder of it all.

Among them was a dapper schoolteacher from a small Kootenay town. With his sleek black-and-silver cigarette holder clenched between his teeth, sporting a smartly tailored suit, he stood out from his colleagues like Noel Coward at a preachers' convention. Robert Sommers was calm, self-assured, seemingly not overawed by his sudden transformation from educator and occasional musician to member of the legislative assembly (MLA).

While few others apart from Bennett and Rolston had thought through their roles and ambitions in the legislature, Sommers knew exactly what he wanted. He coveted one of the most powerful posts in B.C.—that of forests minister—knowing that it was the key portfolio in a province where money from timber, pulp, and paper filled government coffers.

Prior to the election, Bennett, the pragmatic hardware-store owner from Kelowna in the Okanagan Valley, had known little about Robert Sommers, the likeable man from Rossland-Trail in the Kootenays. Tall, with dark hair and handsome, chiselled features, Sommers was charming and articulate, his public posture honed by years in the classroom as a schoolteacher, on stage as a trumpet player and

When the Socreds first came to power in British Columbia in 1952, there were 48 seats in the legislature and they held only 19 of them. It was more than they had ever expected to win as members of a new party with no record and an untried platform, but it was not really enough to govern. Still, they gathered for a legislative session in the spring of 1953, posing for photos with the opposition MLAs. By June there was another election, which the Socreds took with resounding success, increasing their number of seats to 28 and taking 45.5 percent of the popular vote.

performer, and on political platforms in small Interior towns. Sommers was a long-time member of the Social Credit Party at a time when there were few of them. Unlike most of the other MLAs, including Bennett, Sommers had seen the Socred light when it first dawned in Alberta in 1935, becoming an organizer for the party in B.C. Sommers also had educational qualifications as a schoolteacher that most of his new colleagues lacked. Born in Alberta of German immigrant parents, his credentials were solid.

As Bennett looked over his limited pickings for cabinet posts, he knew that Sommers was an obvious choice in a somewhat lacklustre group, but as he studied his colleague he hesitated to make a final decision. Bennett had a blueprint for the future, and the man from the Kootenays didn't seem to fit. Sommers didn't hold to all the tenets of the committed conservative Socreds. He was far removed from the zealous, churchgoing, teetotal majority that formed the core of the party. He didn't spurn the demon rum nor recoil from the evil tentacles of gambling. In fact, he liked both. His music, too, was different from the anthems and hymns of the faithful. He was the swinging, hot-lipped leader of a six-piece band that in the 1940s belted out hit-parade favourites at weddings, Legion dances, and school proms in rural communities in southeastern B.C.

His transgressions were well known in Rossland-Trail and for the most part were forgiven by his neighbours. An elementary school principal, Sommers was a favourite with children and parents alike, and his minor frailties were outweighed by his tireless efforts on behalf of the community as president of the Kiwanis and leader of the children's choir. He helped with fund-raising events and provided entertainment for service organizations. His local popularity put him at the top of the polls when he ran for the provincial seat in 1952. At the age of 41, Sommers had stepped into a new, exciting life in the provincial capital. It was a role he savoured, perhaps too much.

Sommers was an obvious choice for the education ministry, but the new MLA made an impassioned plea to Bennett, asking for the forest portfolio. He promised to mend his heavy-drinking, poker-playing ways if he was given the chance to become minister of lands, mines, and forests. He promised his energies would be dedicated to the support of the government and to Bennett's dream of a wealthy industrialized province that could compete for capital and new markets with other affluent regions on a national and international scale. Bennett took a look at Sommers' assets and liabilities and was inclined to believe that the handsome trumpet player's support of the party and his promises to reform were sincere.

Somewhat ironically, Bennett, still waiting to be confirmed as B.C.'s new premier, took Sommers' word and told him he would get the forest portfolio. W.A.C. had never seen his new colleague's poker parlour countenance but on gaining his prize, tree-lord-in-waiting Bob Sommers wore the face of a man who had won his bluff with a pair of eights.

The Bennett Strategy

If he hesitated to give Sommers the forest portfolio, Bennett won the premiership of the province by taking advantage of political upheaval, making an accurate assessment of the public mood, and capitalizing on every opportunity that presented itself. The non-drinking, non-smoking, staid, dark-suited, 52-year-old businessman didn't look like someone who would take chances, but appearances were deceiving. Bennett's gaming room was the entire province, far grander than Sommers' green-felt poker table. In pursuit of the premiership he never flinched from bucking the odds if the gamble was worth it.

A native of New Brunswick, one of five children, Bennett headed west and worked in the hardware business in Edmonton after the First World War. He moved on to the B.C. Interior in the early 1930s and opened his own store. Despite the Depression that shuttered many small enterprises, his shrewd, entrepreneurial approach enabled him to carve out his own empire in the Okanagan, and it served him well when he made his move into politics.

W.A.C.'s first run for elected office dated back to 1937. On this first attempt he was turned down for the provincial Tory nomination in the South Okanagan. From the beginning Bennett was a conservative, and despite the fact that he did not run, he must have been pleased by the party's comeback that year.

B.C. politics had taken a sudden turn in 1933 when the Conservative Party was wiped out, the Liberals under Duff Pattullo took 34 of the 48 seats, and the newly formed socialist Co-operative Commonwealth Federation (CCF) surprised most electors by taking seven seats and becoming the official opposition. The Liberals won again in 1937, but the Conservative comeback put that party in the role of opposition with eight seats to the CCF's seven.

An ageing Liberal government found itself in a minority position in 1941, with 21 seats to the CCF's 14 and the Tories 12. With the war raging in Europe, there were discussions about forming a coalition government for the duration. Pattullo resisted, but the Japanese attack on Pearl Harbour in December 1941 decided the issue promptly. The coalition was formed, the Liberals having five cabinet seats and the Conservatives three, with the CCF in opposition. Pattullo resigned, and Liberal John Hart became premier. Hart led the Coalition to an easy election win in 1945, taking 37 of the seats to the CCF's 10. There was also one Independent.

W.A.C. Bennett was a tireless promoter of his Okanagan constituency and the apples that grew there. Not content with one successful crop, and despite the fact that he never drank wine, Bennett was instrumental in introducing the wine industry to the area in the 1950s. Within twenty years it became world renowned. He was also responsible for encouraging development of the PGE Railway, the Peace River and Columbia River power projects, and the natural gas industry of the northeast.

Bennett took the political plunge for the second time in 1941, this time winning the Conservative nomination and the seat in a general election. Following Pearl Harbour he became a member of the Coalition government under Hart. Bennett was a hard-working backbencher, although initially not particularly noteworthy. He found that the Coalition government got bogged down in debate, and he became fed up with the inactivity, the lack of vision, and almost everything that was happening or not happening in the House. In an effort to do something about the situation, he ran for the provincial Conservative leadership in 1946, losing out to Herbert Anscomb. The shiny, red, Okanagan apples that he gave to convention delegates were tasty but no match for the polished machine of his opponent. Bennett remained unhappy with the Liberal-Conservative Coalition.

The ties that had bound the parties together in wartime, however, were fraying in peacetime. Ideologies clashed and a power struggle developed as the two parties waged an internal war. Bennett, watching the confrontations with increasing frustration and disgust, bailed out of provincial politics in 1948 to run as a Conservative for the federal riding of Yale. He lost again, but bounced back in the 1949 B.C. election, re-entering the provincial scene as a South Okanagan Conservative MLA in the Coalition government of Liberal Byron "Boss" Johnson.

Nothing had changed in the House, and Bennett's frustration continued to grow. He was an impatient man at the best of times and became more vocal in his criticism as time passed, particularly when he felt that essential business was delayed and distorted by parliamentary procedure and wrangling. Consequently, it was not a surprise when he crossed the floor to sit as an independent member during the 1951 session. His Tory colleagues in the Coalition were outraged. Their anger boiled over when he also talked Tilly Rolston, a Conservative soulmate and 65-year-old Vancouver grandmother, into quitting the party and crossing to sit with him as an Independent. The Tories had hoped to make gains in their own name in the election that would soon be called. The two defections hurt their chances.

In the following months there was conjecture about what the rebel Bennett would do next. Only one thing was clear: his political ambition was growing. Bennett knew the public wanted change, but what changes were possible? Where could he gain votes? The socialist CCF was the opposition in a highly unionized province. It could make significant gains if the right-wing vote developed a serious split, but the Coalition members, particularly the Liberals, felt the CCF could be beaten off. Both Liberals and Tories were preparing this time to go it alone, hoping to win a majority.

To help counter the CCF threat, the Coalition introduced a new voting system. Voters would be asked to select candidates on a preferential basis, making first, second, third, and additional choices according to the number of candidates in a riding. A winner needed 50 percent of the total to take a seat. If there was no one with 50 percent, the leading contender could add second-choice votes to his total in an effort to top the 50 percent requirement. Third choices and subsequent votes would be counted if necessary. The old-line parties believed most people would make Liberals or Tories their first and second choices, but they made two mistakes. They failed to recognize just how much the voters held their parties in contempt, and they never dreamed another credible right-wing party would enter the race and quickly become a contender.

By the late 1940s, the coalition of Conservatives under Herbert Anscomb (left) and Liberals under Byron Johnson, with Johnson as premier, had become an uncomfortable marriage of convenience as the need for joint government faded. When the 1952 election loomed, the two leaders and their parties began jockeying for position and for sole control of the province.

Bennett saw the unique opportunity, but time was short. Waiting in the wings was the Social Credit Party, a right-wing group that had taken provincial power in Alberta in 1935. Social Credit was based on an odd philosophy espoused by an Englishman, Clifford Douglas, who developed a complex monetary policy and had a tendency towards totalitarianism. Few could fathom his financial theories, and in fact they were never introduced in Canada, but in Alberta the right-wing message suited the times, and the party's local leader, William Aberhart, had the fervour and charisma to carry the party to victory. Since then, Social Credit had gained solid support in Alberta and had begun funding and assisting the growth of riding associations in B.C. Among the early organizers was Robert Sommers.

Bennett toyed with his political foes and the news media as they pressed him to reveal his affiliation for the next election. Finally on December 6, 1951, he announced in Kelowna that he had become a card-carrying member of the Social Credit Party. For his South Okanagan constituency it was a triple play. They sent Bennett to Victoria in 1949 as a Tory in the Coalition government. Nine months into 1951 he deserted the government and became an independent member. Now he was in the Social Credit camp, with the government in its death throes and a general election only months away.

Like most nominal Socreds, Bennett never subscribed to the founder's "funny money" theories. Social Credit was for him a vehicle to be used in his appeal to the small-town conservatism of people like himself. He hoped to attract the dissatisfied—and there were lots of them—and to encourage as much of the electorate as possible to cross party lines and make a fresh start free of the baggage, squabbling, and growing ineffectiveness that had characterized the Coalition. From the outset, Bennett maintained he led a "humble little movement," never a political party. He had only a slim chance, but he correctly read all the signs that the public wanted change. Social Credit was unknown but at least unstained in provincial politics. Could voters be swayed to take a gamble?

Following a raucous spring session of the legislature, the increasingly beleaguered Premier Johnson decided to call an election. He dissolved parliament on April 10 and set the polling date for June 12. The Liberals, Conservatives, CCF, and Socreds each planned to run a full slate of candidates. The CCF was sure Bennett would further split the right-wing vote, and its members could hardly suppress their optimism. Their futures had never looked better.

Socred Dawning

"O God Our Help in Ages Past" rang lustily through a jam-packed New Westminster school hall on April 26, 1952, as the rapidly growing B.C. Social Credit Party met in convention. Political pros said they would need a lot more than divine help against their veteran opponents, but the more than 1,100 people in the steamy hall seemed as high as their hopes. They sang, whistled, cheered, booed, heckled, stamped their feet, and fought with each other over details. Reporters described it as a convention that was part politics, but more like a religious revival meeting. The crowd, which included 734 voting delegates, had never before experienced anything like it. Religion overlay all the proceedings. One man declared that it would be sacrilegious to utter the word "politics" at the session. Many people in the province, even those outside the party, shared his view.

Among the odd happenings at the convention was an announcement that boomed over the public address system. A disembodied voice asked if anyone present had a dictionary. Why the request was made was never explained. A few minutes later the same voice wanted to know if there was a lawyer in the house. Normally at a political convention this would trigger a stampede like the Klondike gold rush, but this time no one hurried forward. It is interesting to speculate whether the two calls were related.

Ignoring the hoopla, but keenly watching and waiting for major decisions was Bennett, the Socred-come-lately. While some labelled him an opportunist, he had worked hard to make friends and supporters and was regarded as a front-runner for leadership. Bob Sommers watched with him.

A delegation of Socreds from Alberta attended the meeting with the intention of dictating to British Columbians how the election campaign was to be run. If the B.C. party wanted more financial help and manpower, it would have to dance to Alberta's tune. Some delegates bristled when they heard the ultimatum. And the Albertans' strategy seemed absurd. They proposed the party go into the next election with a campaign chairman but without a leader. The leader would be selected after the provincial vote was decided. Political pros monitoring the meeting scoffed, maintaining voters would never accept such a grab bag. Carried away with their new-found enthusiasm, however, the delegates bought the proposition.

"Big Brother Alberta" had even brought along the man for the job of campaign chairman. He was Reverend Ernest Hansell, MP for Macleod, Alberta, and the Social Credit national president, a pompous, humourless bigot who had raised a national storm four years earlier by dubbing 200 prominent Canadians traitors or communists because of their liberal views.

Bennett played his hand carefully, declining to run against Hansell for the leadership role. The Albertan intoned a left-handed compliment, suggesting that Bennett's stature was "greater than I expected." Declaring that becoming premier of B.C. was the furthest thing from his mind, Hansell later reopened the door slightly when the party began to do much better than anybody expected it would.

It was a bizarre move on the part of the Albertans, but Bennett knew it was playing to his strength. If the Socreds won a few seats in the election, he would be in a prime spot to become leader and have something to build on. If they were annihilated, the blame could be dumped handily on Hansell and the Alberta Socreds' strategy.

Delegates also agreed with the Alberta proposition that the party leader would be chosen by the vote of candidates who were successful in the upcoming election. Few imagined that in three months' time this would mean the selection of the province's next premier. Bennett could dream with the best of them, but it is doubtful that even he entertained this flight of fancy that was to become a reality.

Bennett concentrated his efforts on the first step: getting re-elected in his riding as a Socred. He campaigned tirelessly in his home town and the Okanagan Valley, but virtually passed up the higher profile Lower Mainland. It soon became evident that Bennett's assessment was close to the mark. There were changes coming. At a Vancouver rally, Alberta Premier Ernest C. Manning (father of Preston Manning, who later founded the Reform Party and became leader of the federal opposition in Ottawa in 1997) drew a crowd of 5,000 people to an enthusiastic meeting. At the same time, Robert Sommers, the smoothest and most articulate of the B.C. candidates, was drawing good turnouts in Rossland-Trail.

Other Socred candidates were largely a ragtag collection of political nobodies, but Bennett was undaunted by the scorn of his opponents and critics in the press, particularly those in Vancouver and Victoria. He knew his sprawling province well and recognized the unhappiness and desire for change that existed, particularly outside Vancouver.

June 13 was the most confusing day in B.C.'s frequently confusing political life. The day after casting their votes, the public was told in news reports that only one of the 212 candidates seeking the 48 seats had been elected. Receiving more than 50 percent of the vote in his riding was Ken Kiernan, a Fraser Valley Socred. The multiple-choice vote produced nothing but confusion. The first count showed the Socreds leading in 13 ridings, the CCF in 21, the Liberals in 9, and the Tories in 3. The one and only Independent Labour candidate in the race, Tom Uphill, was also leading. The next day Bennett and four others, two Socreds and two CCFers, were confirmed as winners, but a slow count had delayed the announcement. Sommers led handily in Rossland-Trail but didn't have the necessary 50 percent.

The result might be uncertain, but B.C.'s political future for the next 40 years was taking shape. It was to be a battle between the CCF, later to change its name to the New Democratic Party, and the Socreds. The death knell for Liberals and Conservatives was sounding. Premier Boss Johnson and Tory leader Herbert Anscomb both went down to defeat in the second count. The process was glacially slow.

As vote counting continued, hopes soared for CCF leader 46-year-old Harold Winch, the candidate in Vancouver East, who sat in the legislature with his father, Ernie, a respected, veteran socialist and

Burnaby MLA for several years. Harold was leading in a tight race. Fearful of vote tampering, the CCF mounted its own guards over the ballot boxes in Winch's riding, waiting for the next round. The uncertainty brought a new twist to the streets of the major cities, and bookies got into the act, giving odds and taking bets on the outcome of the undecided votes.

On July 5 the CCF learned it had elected 14 and was leading in 6 ridings; Socreds had elected 15 and were leading in 2; Liberals had elected 2 and were leading in 4; and the Conservatives had elected 2 and were leading in 2. Tom Uphill won his seat.

A few days later, Tory dissidents met to vent their anger at the party's dismal showing and leadership.

By July 8 the scene changed again as another count brought in voters' other choices. Results showed the CCF with 15 elected, leading in 4; Socreds with 15 elected, leading in 3. A nail-biting announcement the next day revealed Socreds and CCF in a dead heat, each with 16 elected, leading in 2. On July 14 it was over. The Socreds had elected 19 and the CCF 18. When the writs were returned July 31 they showed the Liberals with 6 and the Conservatives with 4.

The nineteen Socred winners attended their first meeting together on July 15 in the Hotel Vancouver. It was time to elect a leader under the terms of the resolution approved at the April convention. They were elated and a bit bewildered by their sudden ascension to power. Bennett moved quickly into the driver's seat. He was self-possessed and assured. Despite his various switches of allegiance in the recent past, Bennett had scored a convincing win in his own riding and pulled other winners along on his coattails. He was not the man the Alberta Socreds had hoped for; he was not a compliant politician looking for direction, and Hansell and his followers returned to Alberta with mixed feelings. The initial surmise by some outsiders that Bennett would be his own man was deadly accurate. The leadership session didn't have an opening hymn and it was no contest. Bennett won easily, taking 14 of the 19 votes.

The newspapers ran pictures of Bennett being carried shoulder high by smiling, happy supporters, and they described the unlikely winner for readers who knew little about him. He was five feet, nine inches tall, a chubby 190 pounds, generally known by his initials W.A.C. or as Cec, a New Brunswick native who came to B.C. in 1930 and prospered with a chain of hardware stores in Kelowna, Westbank, Penticton, and Vernon. He had a rapid-fire speaking style, and his

Harold Winch, a self-described proletarian Marxist, was a longshoreman and a bricklayer before being elected to the B.C. legislature in the 1930s. He became leader of the Co-operative Commonwealth Federation in 1939 at the age of 32, and led the party for the next fourteen years, all of them in opposition. He and his fellow CCFers were sure they would win the 1952 election, but there was a new voting system and a new party on the horizon. Winch had no use for Bennett, viewing his party-switching as unprincipled, and said in one debate, "He's W.A.C., and W.A.C. is Wacky." The nickname stuck.

staccato bursts became very familiar to the public over the next twenty years.

Although defeated, Boss Johnson was in no hurry to turn in his resignation. During the anxious wait, Social Credit members fumed and a broken-hearted Winch and his party looked at recount possibilities. Many strategies were discussed because of the razor-thin, one-seat minority victory for Bennett's party. The CCF filed for a recount, but it failed to alter the result. Members were hurt and angry, almost despondent, because they knew they would have won for the first time if it had been a traditional election without the multiple-choice voting system.

Bennett waited impatiently in Victoria, the man of the hour without the reins. On August 1, 1952, Johnson quit, and within hours the merchant from Kelowna was sworn in as B.C.'s 25th premier.

The era of Bennett and Social Credit had arrived in B.C. Critics said the Kelowna upstart would have a very short run and would be demolished in the next election. They claimed voters had been confused by the new system and would understand the ramifications better the next time at the ballot box. All of them were wrong.

In With the New

Bennett formed his cabinet in the face of scathing criticism. Opponents contended he had run nothing more than a hardware store, that he was a mere nails-and-paint salesman, a country hick who could hardly be expected to run a province. He was badly under-estimated, partly because he was a poor speaker and lacked a warm public personality. In public life he appeared hard and calculating, and he often played the devil's advocate in order to spur debate, but face to face or in a small group he was convincing and impressed those close to him with his sincerity. He could be emotional, even shy, with those who mattered to him. He was close to his family and a few trusted friends but did not have a large circle of acquaintances or associates.

What Bennett did have was a driving ambition and a plan. It was a plan that would disarm the Liberal and Conservative parties for decades to come. He had over the years developed big dreams for the future. They were dreams of provincial growth, prosperity, and power; music, literature, and the arts played little part in his life. He was a bottom-line visionary.

As Bennett assessed his options in naming his first cabinet, he faced a number of problems, but two were outstanding. While today's governments are up to their ipso factos in lawyers, Bennett didn't have one legal man, nor did he have an experienced financial expert. He filled these holes by putting two unelected men in his cabinet as attorney general and as finance minister, quickly creating by-elections for them.

Robert Bonner, a smooth, urbane, prematurely balding 31-year-old, was an up-and-coming Vancouver lawyer and prominent Conservative. Bonner had nominated Bennett for leader of the provincial Conservative Party in October 1950, but nevertheless was amazed when the new premier approached him with an offer to become attorney general in the new Socred government. The persuasive Bennett needed a fast answer and got Bonner's yes. It was an astute move. The ex-Tory was to hold the post for nearly all of his sixteen years in government. He eventually resigned to take the top job at MacMillan Bloedel. Throughout the Socreds' twenty years in power, the government's direction was formulated almost entirely by the premier, who shaped the party into the mould he wanted. During much of that time, Bonner was one of the few to have a major influence on government policy.

Robert Bonner's credentials brought some much-needed credibility to the Socreds. He had a distinguished Second World War record. An officer in the Seaforth Highlanders, he had been badly wounded in the Allies' advance up the Italian mainland. On the day

Former army officer, lawyer, and Conservative Party member, Robert Bonner joined the Socreds at the request of his friend W.A.C. Bennett. Along with Bennett and Robert Sommers, he bore the brunt of the attacks from Gordon Gibson and the Liberals during the Sommers affair.

he accepted Bennett's offer, he was unaware he would face as much verbal shot and shell from the opposition benches as he had live ammunition on the war front. Often battered and bruised, Bonner always fought back. When he said yes to Bennett, he had no inkling that the affable Bob Sommers was to be his nemesis, leaving scars on his own credibility and proving more dangerous to his own and the party's future than any adversary on the opposition benches.

Bennett's choice for finance minister was a former Albertan who had been his regular tennis partner when he lived in Edmonton. Einar Gunderson, 53, was an accountant who had held key posts in Alberta's finance department and was well respected in his profession. He and Bennett had kept up their friendship when Gunderson moved to Vancouver after the war. He started his own accounting business, with offices in both Vancouver and Victoria. Like Bonner, Gunderson was surprised at Bennett's offer of a cabinet post. He was known to have Liberal leanings, and a signed photograph of Prime Minister Louis St. Laurent hung on his office wall. After the initial surprise, however, he took Bennett's offer and, like Bonner, prepared to run in a by-election, but his stint as finance minister and MLA was short-lived. He won the by-election but lost in the 1953 general election. Over the long reign of the Social Credit government he provided advice to the premier, who himself filled the role of finance minister after Gunderson's demise.

Because the race had been so close, Bennett's claim that he was the new premier caused problems for B.C.'s lieutenant governor,

Einar Gunderson was a short-term politician, winning a by-election but losing in the 1953 general election and yet another by-election that W.A.C. Bennett set up for the man he wanted as his finance minister. Gunderson, an accountant who had known Bennett in Alberta, remained the financial adviser and confidant of the premier for the remainder of the Bennett era. He was a controversial appointee to various high-profile provincial boards.

Clarence Wallace. Social Credit, with nineteen members, was in a minority position, and the CCF under Harold Winch had only one seat less. Winch contended that he could win enough support from the eleven others elected to give him more overall strength than the Socreds and the right to form a government. He felt there was a strong "anybody but Bennett" undercurrent. Wallace decided to interview the eleven other MLAs. He got vague responses from nearly all of them as to whether they would support Bennett or the socialist leader in the House.

Wallace sought outside advice on what he knew was a tricky constitutional issue. The learned judges he consulted had differing views. The lieutenant governor even trekked to Ottawa to discuss the issue with Prime Minister St. Laurent, who didn't help, telling Wallace the decision was his.

In Victoria, Bennett pressed his case. He argued that B.C. had been without effective government long enough, and refusal to let him form one would lead to greater chaos. Wallace, a well-respected man of principle, studied all the options and finally agreed.

The ten men and one woman who constituted Bennett's first cabinet marched into Government House for the swearing in. Many thought the eleven would have more success as a soccer team than a provincial cabinet. Two key men, lawyer Robert Bonner and accountant Einar Gunderson, were without seats. Tilly Rolston, conservative businesswoman and grandmother, stood beside a gospel-singing evangelist who was developing a taste for fast cars and planes.

One minister was a streetcar driver, another a farmer, and yet another a garage and repair-shop owner. The minister of municipal affairs and provincial secretary was Wesley Black. Bonner became attorney general, and Gunderson, finance minister. Public works went to evangelist Phil Gaglardi; agriculture to Ken Kiernan; labour to Lyle Wicks; railways, trade, industry, and fisheries to Ralph Chetwynd; and health and welfare to Eric Martin. Tilly Rolston, the Tory who had crossed the floor to sit with Bennett and the only female Socred MLA, was named minister of education, and Robert Sommers became the new minister of lands, mines, and forests, exactly what he had wanted and begged for.

The often ebullient Bennett was constrained by the ceremony and gravity of the moment. He spoke briefly, stressing his government would be neither left nor right but "a middle of the road government." Bennett's lack of a discernible political philosophy frustrated his provincial opponents and every federal government for the next twenty years. He wandered all over the lanes from his "middle of the road," and tackling Bennett's readily adaptable pragmatism and unabashed filching of anyone else's good ideas was like trying to pin down one of his silver-lined clouds. He never hesitated to say he had changed his mind, the switch well coated in bafflegab, leaving the former position bobbing and hopefully forgotten as he took a new tack. He never believed in long explanations—then was then, now is now.

Years later Bennett confessed he always knew that among his MLAs he had a "few squirrels in the basement." For two decades, however, he was a master manipulator of power who battled both the right and left of the political spectrum, his confidence unassailable. He didn't quail when events blew up in his face, and as Robert Sommers would prove, his bravado let him coolly ride over scandals and crises.

Frequent foe Stu Keate, publisher of the *Victoria Times* and later the *Vancouver Sun*, believed from the outset that Bennett was an opportunistic menace to Keate's traditional Liberal beliefs and not the buffoon that some argued. Keate advised, "The image of this man as a small-town hardware merchant is illusory. William Andrew Cecil Bennett is as astute and tough a politician as has ever appeared on the Canadian scene ... Every time he leaves Victoria, Vancouver Island rises a foot."

Critics scoffed at Bennett's first cabinet, but many of its members proved effective and durable, remaining in cabinet for several years. They are, left to right: Phil Gaglardi, Ralph Chetwynd, Ken Kiernan, Tilly Rolston, Einar Gunderson, W.A.C. Bennett, Robert Bonner, Wesley Black, Robert Sommers, Lyle Wicks, and Eric Martin.

The Vision

During the war years, Bennett was one of the MLAs appointed to the Post-War Rehabilitation Council, a position that provided him with the perfect background from which to develop his ideas about the future of Canada's westernmost province. The purpose of the Council was to study B.C.'s place in a new and different world. As a member, Bennett travelled to the far corners of the province, where he saw sparsely populated, undeveloped land. He envisioned huge farms in the northeast, and forest and mining development in the northwest and the southeast. Some of the future potential of the province was obvious, some was hidden, but Bennett quickly appreciated that the future lay in the development of not just Vancouver, the Lower Mainland, and Vancouver Island, but also the enormous land mass to the east and the north, a mass so large it could easily swallow the states of Washington and Oregon or take in both Britain and France.

The council's interim report, tabled in the legislature in 1943, called for development of a steel industry, extension of the Pacific Great Eastern Railway (PGE) into the Peace River area, increased development of agriculture, and further exploitation of the forest and mining sectors. Also recommended was public ownership of the hydro-electric authority, something Bennett was to act on at a later date, much to the surprise of opposing politicians and the public, when he nationalized the B.C. Electric Company in 1961.

By 1950, industrialization in the Lower Mainland, which had boomed during the war, was stagnating and Bennett began promoting the Rehabilitation Council's recommendations. He believed diversification must wait until primary resources had provided the funds for a badly needed transportation system that would open up the Interior and the north to provincial, federal, and foreign capital investment.

The coast, the islands, and the valleys and mountains of the hinterland were covered by a seemingly endless carpet of green ranging from the giant Douglas firs and cedars of the coast to the smaller spruce, pine, and fir of the Interior and the north. At that time there were about 1.3 million people in B.C., and some 32,000 were employed directly in the forests, the sawmills, and pulp mills. Many times that number earned their wages in spinoff companies as manufacturers, mechanics, truckers, trainmen, tugboat crews, scalers, sales staff, and office workers.

Bennett understood the value of the trees, but he also noticed signs for concern. There were sinister stirrings in the forests. Small loggers complained they were being forced out by monopolies and big money that had moved in after the introduction of Forest Management Licences in 1948. Unions were uneasy, suspicious of the changes they saw coming. Mechanization and technology were making inroads and eliminating traditional jobs. New improved saws and milling machines had replaced double-bladed axes and ten-foot crosscut saws to bring down the forest giants and produce lumber faster and better. There were increasing cries for better management.

Bennett was aware that unless he handled the issues adroitly, a raging public and political fire could burst into flames and consume everything in its path, including his fledgling administration.

Did Bennett have the time, the people, the ideas, and the ability to convince British Columbians he was the man to develop the province for coming generations? The party had only 34 percent of the almost 700,000 votes cast in the summer of 1952. Would his dream turn into mission impossible? The people he had selected for his cabinet could make the difference.

Top-Hat Time

W.A.C. Bennett carefully planned his strategy for the first session of his new government, one he knew wouldn't last long. The defeat of his minority administration was a foregone conclusion, but in the time available he intended to work on the issues that had the most vote-getting appeal.

Bennett was a fashion plate in shiny top hat and morning coat when Lieutenant Governor Wallace arrived on February 3, 1953, to open the 23rd session of the legislature. The Socreds were six seats short of a majority, but they exuded all the confidence in the world. The Speech from the Throne promised everything from elimination of hospital care payments to tougher treatment for the Sons of Freedom Doukhobors in the Kootenays. That move alone gained Bennett many friends. At the time the Sons were seen as outrageous zealots, a 2,500-member radical Russian religious sect that burned houses, placed bombs, refused to send its children to school, and staged nude parades in its battles with authorities.

The Throne Speech also announced a royal commission to revamp liquor laws, as demanded by a majority of the electorate. While many of his Bible-belt colleagues and other Socred Party adherents disagreed with these reforms, and though Bennett himself was a teetotaller, he introduced changes that would expand liquor sales and bring more money to government coffers. Bennett was also instrumental in introducing the wine industry to the Okanagan in the 1960s—a major economic player in the region to this day—because it meant jobs and growth. During his early political career, Bennett saw what booze could do to politicians, making them ineffective and easily corrupted (he had feared Sommers might be one of these), and his closest friends were those who drank little and so could be trusted. One of those close friends, Waldo Skillings, once observed that Bennett was never a lady's man but often admired religious, righteous, non-drinking, God-fearing women.

After the Throne Speech, the Socreds got down to the day-to-day business of government. After fighting off opposition demands for a budget for several weeks, Finance Minister Gunderson finally rose in

Everyone knew the session that started on February 3, 1953, would not last long, as the Socreds needed Liberal or Tory support to survive. Bennett's political acumen was in evidence for the first time as his government lasted for more than a month, enough time to give the public a taste of his party's policy and direction—a taste the public obviously liked.

the house on February 18 to present the only economic forecasts he would ever make in his short career as an MLA. He proposed a balanced budget of $175 million for 1953-54. Gunderson gave minor breaks to the little guy. He raised the limit for a meal without taxes from 50 cents to a dollar and cut the cost of a car licence by 10 percent, a saving of $1.60 and $2.50 for small and large cars. There were some increased taxes for big business, including a 10 percent profit tax on the forest and mining industries. This was crafted to exclude the small operator who made a profit of $25,000 or less. If the vested interests complained, so much the better; it was all good publicity for Bennett as he rolled out a shrewd blueprint for the future.

Bennett's twenty-year assault on "union bosses" was also launched. His new labour minister, Lyle Wicks, announced that of the 2.8 million working days lost to strikes in Canada the previous year, B.C. alone accounted for about a third: 869,000 days. He said changes to the labour code were coming. An early *Vancouver Sun* headline also heralded the beginning of Bennett's lifelong war with Ottawa: "B.C. Will Demand New Deal; Millions More From Ottawa."

As predicted, the minority government fell quickly. It went down to defeat in the legislature on March 24, 1953, by 28 votes to 17 over a government bill aimed at giving rural areas a better deal in education financing. W.A.C. had chosen the sequence in which he played his cards, and the defeat was of Bennett's choosing. He knew he was riding high in public opinion, his strength lay in the small towns and farming communities, and this bill was introduced specifically for this favoured constituency. The opposition knew this as well and offered to deal with other bills on the agenda first. Bennett turned them down and so engineered his own defeat and the next election. He charged that the opposition had ganged up on him before he could unveil all his plans. The Socreds had been in power for about eight months.

The Liberals, smarting badly from the 1952 election, made many inaccurate assessments of Bennett. Leader E.T. Kenney, who would actually resign before the election, made one of the first: "I predict that this government will go down as the most inept and inert in history."

A new election was not called immediately because CCF leader Harold Winch again went to Lieutenant Governor Wallace, contending that he should be allowed to form a government. He still believed he could get support from several non-Socred members. Winch's hopes died when Kenney said his Liberals would never support a CCF government.

Clarence Wallace (left), the first B.C. lieutenant governor born in the province, served in the First World War and returned home to his destined career with the Wallace family's Vancouver shipyards. He became lieutenant governor in 1951, and the 1952 election put him in a difficult position. A one-seat advantage following an election had not occurred before in B.C. history, and although he sought advice from every available source, he found the final decision to be his alone. He gave the nod to Bennett and the new Social Credit Party.

It was the end of a long dream. The shattered Winch announced he was "tired" and offered his resignation to the party. Within the CCF ranks there were no pleas for him to stay. Over the years a drinking problem had grown worse with his frustration at being denied the crown he felt was his, and after twenty years in opposition he was disillusioned and finished. The name Harold Winch, once a sure-fire socialist vote-getter in B.C., was not to be heard again in Victoria. He later ran and was elected a member of Parliament for his home riding of Vancouver East, but his Ottawa career was undistinguished and plagued again by heavy drinking. Arnold Webster, a schoolteacher without much charisma or political experience, replaced Winch as CCF leader.

In the 1953 election campaign, the Liberals were led by former MP Arthur Laing, who had returned from Ottawa for the fight. Deane Finlayson, a handsome, dashing, RCAF flyer turned real estate salesman, headed the Tories. It was possibly a braver move than anything Finlayson did in wartime. The provincial Conservatives were in terrible shape and have remained so ever since. In 1953 they couldn't muster a full slate, falling eight candidates short for the 48 ridings.

British Columbians went into a general election with more alternatives than they had ever had before, but with less awareness of the new leaders' qualities and policies than they would have liked. Bennett, despite the short stint in office, remained the leader of a new, still unproven party whose strong suit was that it had to be better than what went before.

The June 9 election was again fought under the multiple-choice voting system, but the drama from a year earlier was missing. The electorate decided Bennett deserved another chance. This time it was a cakewalk for the Socreds, who took 28 seats and 45.5 percent of the vote. Sommers was an easy winner. The CCF picked up 14 seats, 29 percent of the vote; the Liberals 4 seats, 23.36 percent; and the Conservatives one, 1.11 percent. "Untouchable" Tom Uphill came through once again as the Independent Labour member. The lone Tory, Larry Giovando, soon left that party without representation in the House when he became unhappy with its performance and bolted to sit as a second Independent.

A surprising casualty was Finance Minister Einar Gunderson, the man for whom Bennett had created a by-election. Ironically it was a fellow accountant, Archie Gibbs, who gave the Liberals Gunderson's Oak Bay (Victoria) riding. Arthur Laing won Vancouver Point Grey at the expense of Tilly Rolston. Bennett was saddened by the defeat of the woman who had crossed the floor to join him as an Independent and as a Socred. He was one of the few who knew she was fighting cancer, which soon claimed her life. Finlayson, despite his brave campaign performance, lost at the polls, and although he remained leader of the party for some years, he never obtained a seat in the legislature.

Among the four Liberals who won seats was colourful millionaire Gordon Gibson. Some dismissed the burly Gibson as a loud-mouthed, bare-knuckled, roughhouse logger who had become rich. He won in the lumbering district of Lillooet, well to the northeast of Vancouver, where he had championed the small logger, who he felt was being pushed out by the big guys. He had once been an independent logger himself, and he hadn't forgotten, even though he was now a wealthy man. Well versed in the industry, Gibson set his sights, and those of the Liberal Party, on the affairs of forestry and its re-elected minister,

After the 1952 election, Tilly Rolston told a Victoria Times *reporter that her three children "all grew up so quickly...that she found she had too much time to herself. That's when she ran for parks commissioner." Eight years later she entered provincial politics and was a Conservative member of the Coalition government until Bennett persuaded her to cross the floor in 1951. She was the second woman in B.C. to hold a cabinet post. The first was Liberal Mary Ellen Smith, who in 1925 was the first female cabinet minister in the British Empire.*

Bob Sommers. The "Bull of the Woods," a nickname he didn't eschew and the title of his later autobiography, was set to rampage.

Bennett convened the House in September, happily confronting a totally demoralized opposition. Now firmly entrenched, he focused on the big picture. Roads and access were his priorities. He was captivated by the possibilities for the large, lonely, Alberta-abutting, Peace district with its gas and oil potential. He knew hydro power could be harnessed from the majestic, mighty Peace River. He also planned an extension of the PGE Railway, which at the time was a 40-year-old joke in B.C. In 1952 the railway served little purpose and carried next to nothing along its few miles of rusty tracks. It was better known as the "Please Go Easy" or "Prince George Eventually." The line was completed to Prince George in 1952, and its extension into the Peace River country was part of Bennett's grand scheme. The southern extension from Squamish to North Vancouver was scheduled to open in 1956.

With a clear mandate, Bennett soon began to flex his political muscle. He made it abundantly clear that he wanted no interference from Ottawa, particularly with respect to B.C.'s natural resources. In the years ahead Bennett would make some provocative speeches and statements that sometimes led to criticism he was as much a separatist as anyone in Quebec. It was all part of his act: over-exaggeration to make a point, to confuse the opposition, and to please the people of his province. Bennett was a staunch Canadian but a master of the "poor B.C." credo that dated back to the confederation politics of the province's second premier, simple Bill Smith, who changed his name to Amor de Cosmos (Lover of the Universe). Bennett accused Ottawa of trying to tear down his "little government" and stealing money for the federal coffers. It was awful, he moaned, it was "victimization," but he would fight on against the forces of evil.

Bennett also believed B.C. had been wracked too often by its highly unionized labour force. The cold war with Russia was turning very chilly, and he loved to tie the CCF to the "raving commies." Some felt he had a point, as several of B.C.'s powerful unions—the mine-mill, fishermen, electrical workers, and others—had leaders who were avowed communists. Bennett brought in a new Labour Relations Act that gave Labour Minister Lyle Wicks sweeping powers to tackle the seemingly never-ending disputes. Until the end of Bennett's reign, organized labour was an implacable foe. Despite cries that he was grinding them into the ground and reintroducing serfdom, the unions grew and prospered.

Bennett adopted an Alice-in-Wonderland approach to the business of the legislature. He refused to have a Hansard, a verbatim account of debates. He maintained that if members could read later what transpired, their attendance would suffer. His attitude was "Anything I say is what I say it is." If his more extreme comments didn't look so good in print, he denied them and said the press had it all wrong.

While there were times he was genuinely enraged and spitting mad at press coverage, the rest of the time it was fakery and play-acting, loud, headline-making jousting that Bennett loved. His reasoning was sound; people generally believed him more than they did the press. It was only when his government had grown stale and tired after two decades in power that the constant hammering from the media had much effect. In the early days, Wacky, as the papers often called him, rolled over the media without a problem. Reporters at the *Vancouver Sun* used to joke that the paper's blistering editorials before any election—blaming Bennett for everything but the weather—were worth at least another five percentage points for the Socreds at the polls.

This was the era when newspapers dominated reporting; local radio coverage was scanty and television was not yet a universal medium. Bennett's chief foes, *Vancouver Sun* publisher Don Cromie and *Victoria Times* publisher Stu Keate, were rabidly Liberal and made no bones about it. Wacky painted some wonderful scenarios in his attacks. The *Sun* was "just a big city-slicker operation, a marionette

Bennett's commitment to better transportation links in B.C. was evident on September 15, 1954, when he proudly turned the sod at the site of the new Rosedale-Agassiz bridge. At the ceremony were (left to right) Labour Minister Lyle Wicks, Agriculture Minister Ken Kiernan, Bennett, and Highways Minister Phil Gaglardi.

with the Liberals in Ottawa pulling the strings." The *Times* was no better, only smaller.

The *Vancouver Province* and the *Victoria Colonist*, both more conservative in their approach, were what was referred to as family newspapers, and their sympathies sometimes lay with the government. They escaped much of the Socred wrath. Most smaller dailies rallied behind him editorially, particularly when his economic development plans brought money and jobs to their regions.

Bennett bedevilled the Liberal cheerleaders to the end, and the right-wing media to a lesser degree. Until this time, newspaper editors had been accustomed to politicians who found value in cozying up to them, who sought their wise counsel and in return told them the secrets of the day. Bennett put the boots to them every chance he got and usually walked away flashing a broad, phoney-looking smile, which was guaranteed to infuriate his enemies.

Perhaps it was the obvious animosity between the media and Premier Bennett that put reporters hot on the trail of Sommers as soon as they sensed there was a story developing in the legislature.

THE SCANDAL

As the Social Credit Party took power, it faced a great deal of animosity from the old-line parties, particularly the Liberals, who held sway in Ottawa and had been comfortable dealing with their former man in Victoria, Byron "Boss" Johnson. Some Liberals and Conservatives voiced the view that the new party would ruin the country and split the West.

Wisps of Smoke

Forest fires can start in many ways. Some begin suddenly and spectacularly from a lightning strike, one bolt turning thousands of acres into a landscape of ruin. There are other fires that for various reasons start slowly, smouldering silently, giving off only little wisps of smoke before roaring into flames. That was how it was for Bennett and his forests minister during late 1954, with Gordon Gibson ready at any moment to fan the flames.

The trips back and forth between Victoria and his riding in the Kootenays were often long and arduous for Robert Sommers, involving a boat trip to or from Vancouver Island and then a day-long car or bus trip to Castlegar. After the second Socred victory he made a decision that was important for his family, but which stretched his financial resources. His first wife had died years earlier, after giving birth to a daughter who was now grown. He had since remarried and was now the father of two younger children, a boy and a girl. He decided to move his family to Victoria in order to spend more time with them and reduce the number of hours spent travelling back and forth.

Sommers maintained that his first electoral win had left him $900 in debt. It was a debt that continued to grow in Victoria, where the cost of living and buying a house was considerably higher than it had been in the Kootenays.

In 1953, MLAs got a sessional indemnity of $3,000 because the House only sat a few weeks each year. A cabinet minister received another $7,500 for what was a full-time job. It was respectable take-home pay for the time, but not quite enough to provide Sommers with the trappings he viewed as important to his new post. He chose a comfortable home in suburban Victoria, but he was short of money for financing and furnishings.

Ironically, as minister of forests, Sommers held the fortunes of the province's largest companies in his hands. Approval of an FML sent a public company's stock prices soaring, and when stocks rose, shareholders were happy and company presidents received huge bonuses. Sommers was now moving in the moneyed circles of these company presidents, and it made his own shortage of funds more difficult and embarrassing.

One of Sommers' few friends in Victoria or Vancouver was H.W. "Wick" Gray, a minor player on the forestry scene, owner of a small logging company, Pacific Coast Services (PCS). He was a hustler on

Wick Gray was a small mill owner in B.C.'s largest industry, forestry. He had become a friend of Robert Sommers when he hired the schoolteacher's band to play at a company function in the Kootenays. The help Gray offered after Sommers moved to Victoria led to the downfall of both of them.

the fringe of a burgeoning industry. Sommers had first met Gray when his band was hired in the late 1940s to play at an event Gray had sponsored in the Kootenays. Gray frequented the forest industry world that Sommers was now entering, but as a small mill operator he had little influence. Having Sommers as a friend greatly increased his importance in the eyes of one of Vancouver's big forest consulting firms, as well as with the larger company executives who had in the past looked on him as small potatoes.

To help Sommers out of the financial predicament created by his move to Victoria, Gray offered Sommers a loan, the first of several. It was later said to be just a loan from one old friend to another. There was nothing signed, no interest set, no date named for repayment. In another friendly gesture, Wick Gray's company picked up the $607 tab for some East Indian rugs that Bob and Nona Sommers purchased from a Vancouver store for their house in Victoria.

Sommers' immediate problems seemed to be resolved when his old friend Gray came through with the loans, but in fact they were just beginning. The fly in the ointment was that Gray's benevolence was due in part to Charlie Schultz.

Charlie Schultz was the gregarious head of C.D. Schultz and Associates, a highly successful forest-industry consulting firm with a staff of about a hundred and offices in downtown Vancouver. Charlie was a consultant to companies large and small, with employees expert in a dozen different areas of forest management and engineering. He was always on the lookout for good political connections. Gray's relationship with Sommers had a high dollar value because one of

Schultz's preoccupations was an attempt to get FML #22 on Vancouver Island for his client BCFP, E.P. Taylor's forest company.

In late 1954, Sommers made a trip east to attend his daughter's wedding to an American in Detroit. Hector Munro, the 52-year-old president of BCFP and a director of Taylor's much larger Argus Corporation, suggested it would be an opportunity for Sommers to meet and talk to Taylor about forest licence problems, and so a tea party was arranged in Toronto.

One of the invited guests at the wedding was Wick Gray, who picked up a $2,500 cheque from BCFP to help defray his expenses during the trip east, which now included a visit to the Taylor estate for afternoon tea.

It was an impressive backdrop for the meeting, far removed from the dingy rooms frequented by Kootenay service clubs or the local school auditoriums where Sommers' band had played only months earlier. He could not help but be impressed. At the gathering in addition to Sommers, his wife, and Taylor were Hector Munro, several other Argus directors, Wick Gray, and big, abrasive Wallace McCutcheon, E.P.'s right-hand man. It was described later as "a simple get-to-know-each-other meeting while Bob was in the East." The group talked trees and the rejection of BCFP's first FML bid in 1948.

Sommers was no fool; he knew that schoolteachers and trumpet players generally used the back entrance to Taylor's place. He knew it was the power of his forest portfolio that got him through the front door. The effusive welcome, the warm handshakes, and the pandering were a new and heady experience, but Bob was out of his league. In this elegant setting the fledgling politician was probably the most innocent creature in the woods since Red Riding Hood asked the Big Bad Wolf the way to Grandma's house.

The hospitality paid off for Taylor, who made a trip to Victoria in January 1955. The Argus boss made a new pitch for an FML at a meeting in the Empress Hotel. Bennett, Sommers, and Einar Gunderson listened carefully to the BCFP proposal. Although he had lost in the general election and a subsequent by-election, Gunderson was present at Bennett's invitation.

Years later, Bennett would recall this Victoria meeting and emphasize how badly he wanted Taylor's new application to succeed because of the massive investment involved. Taylor was proposing to build a new pulp mill on Vancouver Island that would provide hundreds of jobs along with more tax revenue. While cabinet supposedly made

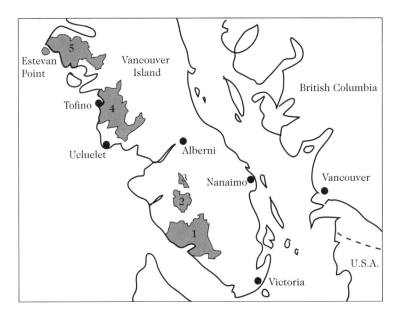

B.C. Forest Products' FML #22 covered over 250,000 acres of land on western Vancouver Island, in five chunks stretching from Port Renfrew to Estevan Point. One of the requirements of the licence was that BCFP build a road that would provide public access to the west coast. The licence caused a storm when it was granted, and it encompassed some areas that became controversial for different reasons in the 1980s and 1990s after BCFP was long gone.

these decisions, it was Bennett who called the tune. He bought Taylor's proposition and told Sommers to cement the deal. Bennett insisted there were no special concessions and recalled, "I'm sure that Sommers didn't give them any special treatment and I didn't ask him to. He dealt with it the same as any other forestry licence."

After Sommers met E.P. Taylor in Toronto, followed by Taylor's meeting with the premier in Victoria, the rumour mills in political and forestry circles began to grind. The talk of FML favouritism was enhanced during late-night card games in the Union Club, where the scotch flowed freely and lots of money changed hands. No one watched and listened to the rumours more carefully than Gordon Gibson, who was mapping out his own agenda.

The Bull of the Woods

It was the biggest, most beautiful, red cedar tree that Gordon Gibson had ever seen, dominating the hillside above a lonely inlet on the west coast of Vancouver Island where he lived and worked for much of his early life. He was intrigued by trees, their size, their beauty, and their usefulness. Despite this affinity, he found no contradiction in cutting them down. They were a crop to be harvested and then replaced by another crop that would grow and mature for future generations. It was the normal life cycle of the forest.

Gibson first saw the magnificent cedar in the early 1920s. It was near Clayoquot Sound, an environmental battleground in the 1990s, but not when Gibson was there. He was working in the woods with his brother Jack when they came upon the tree that soared 225 feet into the sky. Its first giant limbs were 100 feet above the ground. The tree was perfectly symmetrical. "This was the most outstanding tree we had ever seen," Gibson recalled years later. In practical terms it was worth about $1,750 to the two brothers.

The logging business in the early twentieth century was still a world of big-muscled men, double-bladed axes, and wicked crosscut saws with shark-sharp teeth. As the Gibsons studied the magnificent tree, they knew their six-foot saw would be no match for the giant, and they sent for a ten-footer. For a whole day, from dawn to dusk, they sweated and toiled on the hillside, laboriously eating into the girth of that spectacular cedar. Finally there was a crack, the cut widened, and the giant began to sway. Gibson wondered at its magnificence even in death. The Bull was never poetic, but his autobiography states, "It seemed to pause in the air for a moment like an eagle in slow motion."

Gibson had respect for the fallen "eagle," as he had for all the trees and forests of his province and for all the men and women who worked in them, making a lonely, dangerous living in isolated camps along the coast. They were out of touch with the world except for infrequent visits by coastal steamers and, later, by daring young men in their float-equipped flying machines. Roads were few and far between.

Born while his father ventured to Dawson City, part of the Klondike gold rush of 1898, Gibson loved to say he came up from the bottom, but this was not entirely true. His father was a hustling entrepreneur who ensured that his family worked as hard as those he hired for his

Logging in the B.C. woods was a tough and often dangerous job. Before the surge of mechanization in the 1940s and 1950s, it was mostly done by hand, with burly loggers wielding crosscut saws and axes to bring the giants down.

enterprises. Gordon Gibson contended, "We have been called many names in our day, but by God no one has ever said we were lazy. My three brothers and I have been in every kind of business except running liquor or owning a whorehouse." He joked that his only wasted years were from age eight to fourteen when he went to school. After that he went to work in the woods. In the 1920s the Gibson Lumber and Shingle Company produced 20,000 shingles a day in bundles of 100 that sold for five dollars. The Gibsons owned one of the early forest management licences, and the sale of part of it in the 1950s contributed to the family's wealth. The Gibson family empire expanded over the years into other enterprises, most of them, such as transportation and fishing, closely allied to the forest industry, although they also had a licence for a new Vancouver radio station, CKLG.

Gibson cultivated a public image as a hard-working, hard-drinking, hard-living logger who'd made good. In 1953, the lifelong Liberal decided to enter provincial politics in order to support the cause of the small logger. He won the Lillooet seat. Gibson's performance in the House was blunt, direct, and rang with heartfelt conviction. His colourful turn of phrase and late-night antics in the legislature, when his speeches sometimes rambled along the whisky trail, had many laughing and some fuming. There were times in the legislature when heavy drinking—more than a bottle a day before he gave it up— threatened to bring him down. The drink was responsible for many of his more extravagant statements both inside and outside of politics. For years he was ignored as nothing but a playboy, a loud-mouthed, wealthy drunk, although his outlandish escapades were generally forgiven in a land that loves a character. Some opponents attacked him as a buffoon, venting pet peeves, but people who knew him well knew that along with the woodchips, Gibson boasted shrewd business acumen. It was also obvious he was deadly serious and genuinely concerned about the small loggers of the B.C. woods, who he knew well and respected.

Increased mechanization and modernization in the woods were fuelling predictions that the small operator was on the way out. Equipment costs were skyrocketing, but timber companies had to spend the money if they hoped to meet the demands of a rapidly expanding industry. In what seemed an unlimited marketplace, many small companies struggled to find a niche for themselves when it became apparent the times were changing. Others believed the time had come to get out, and they sold their operations and their forest licences to the big companies that had the financial backing to take advantage of new mass-production lumber manufacturing techniques and could also afford to build a new pulp or paper mill.

Although only nineteen FMLs had been awarded in the six years since the system was introduced in 1948, by late 1954 the government had more than twenty new applications for licences under consideration. Natural resource development in the province was exploding, and FMLs were awarded only to large companies willing to build lumber mills and pulp-and-paper mills, and to provide new jobs in exchange for long-term cutting rights in the forests. Under the terms of the royal commission report, the new jobs would be created not only in manufacturing and logging, but also in silviculture, reforestation, and road and bridge construction, as the large companies took over total management of the forests. This type of forest management was new to the province and had only been performed previously, to a much lesser degree, by the forest service. Ministry staff remained responsible for managing some Crown land, the working

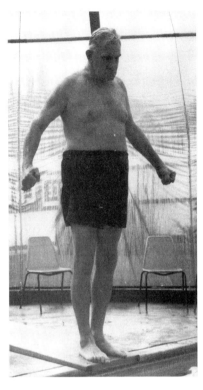

Gordon Gibson was always ready to ham it up for photographers, in this case Victoria's Jim Ryan, and his loud-mouthed, outrageous pronouncements often gained him an audience of well-wishers and antagonists. His buffoonery, however, masked an intelligence and a deep dedication to the small loggers of the province, with whom he felt a great kinship.

circles reserved for the use of small logging companies, but these lands were of poor quality compared to the forests dedicated to FMLs. Sometimes small companies contracted their services to the larger companies, while many independent loggers closed down their operations completely in order to take on higher-paying unionized jobs with the big companies.

The small logger was told either by the big companies or by the forest service where to cut, when to cut, and how much to cut. Loss of a cutting contract with a big firm could put a small operator out of business. Similarly, without a vital FML, a big company had no secure wood supply. In each case the stakes were high, and the system was wide open to payoffs and special favours.

Gibson worried about the growing clout and power of the major companies and fretted at his inability to help the small guy while the government continued to carve up the forests. He knew the industry at all levels and soon heard word on the street that Charlie Schultz had the inside track, that he was the one advising a number of firms on how to obtain a forest licence, and that he had hired Wick Gray as a liaison to the minister's office. How much Gibson knew of Sommers' early involvement with Wick Gray is not clear. What he did know was the importance of the FML that would make the Argus Corporation a much bigger player than it had been previously. That FML was on the west coast of Vancouver Island, an area Gibson knew and loved; it had formerly been his turf.

The Gibson brothers had a float-camp in Chamiss Bay, Nootka Sound, near where they were logging on the west coast of Vancouver Island in the 1940s.

On February 1, 1955, Gibson, who lived in the nearby Embassy Motel during the legislative session, invited Sommers for what became a two-hour dinner meeting. Although political foes, they had some respect for each other, and Gibson asked Sommers for a temporary suspension of new FMLs, particularly on the west coast of Vancouver Island, until some of the systemic problems could be worked out. Sommers refused, adding that new licences were already committed and he knew which companies were going to get them. Although he didn't mention any names during this conversation, the go-ahead had by this time been given to Church Sawmills Ltd., Empire Sawmills, B.C. Forest Products, East Asiatic Company, and the Tahsis Company.

During the meal, Gibson also turned his attention to Sommers' personal problems. The two men travelled in some of the same circles, and Gibson asked Sommers if he was short of money. If he needed a few thousand dollars, Gibson was willing to lend him the money. The Liberal warned the minister not to stick his neck out too far or he could be ruined. He later said that he also told Sommers he could become as bad as the Coalition government for taking payoffs. Sommers told Gibson to mind his own business.

In a fall 1958 interview with *Vancouver Province* reporter Tom Hazlett, Gibson said Sommers told him, "I won't play. We're going to go on issuing licences whether you like it or not." Gibson added, "I said I would talk with the premier and I did so for one and a half hours the next morning. I tried to talk Bennett out of FMLs and I brought out all the evidence now before the courts."

When Bennett dismissed Gibson's disclosures, the stubborn Liberal MLA decided to throw his first punch and raise his charges in the legislature. Only hours later, on February 2, 1955, the opening bell rang on what was to be a bloody, multi-round bout.

The papers reported that Gibson had the "vocal power of a bull elephant" when he accused the government of "fraudulent" handling of forest licences. According to the *Sun*, "The king-sized former logger gave a roaring, finger-shaking, and at times oath-hurtling performance as he kept the Legislature in turmoil." People were left to guess what the oaths were, but they read that the scene resembled a "loggers' weekend spree." Gibson raged on, claiming that Squamish loggers were denied the right to appeal a licence application in their area. A red-faced and furious Bennett was immediately on his feet, yelling at Gibson, until he was told by Speaker Tom Irwin to sit down. Gibson yelled back, "Our forefathers who built this country and the soldiers who laid down their lives for this country would turn over in their graves if sinking to such a low level of public morals is the outcome of their sacrifice."

On the government side of the House, Phil Gaglardi was at his pulpit-pounding best as he screamed "Shame, shame, shame" at Gibson. Bellowing back, Gibson told the pint-sized preacher that he was talking about honesty, "and you can put that in your sermon the next time you preach." Gaglardi, a verbal roof-rattler in his own right, later mused, "I sound like a Zephyr beside a cyclone. He must have made all his money blowing the trees down."

Sommers sniped from the front bench, demanding to know if Gibson had ever made a capital gain, a reference to the profit made from the sale of part of his family's FML. His implication was that Gibson shouldn't be criticizing a system that had made his family so much money—and also that Gibson, a wealthy man, was not in a position to represent the interests of the often financially strapped independent loggers.

The Bull of the Woods charged back, contending some companies and their top executives had made millions in share-price hikes after receiving a licence and before cutting a single tree. The argument in the House died like a sudden squall, but Gibson was far from through.

Thomas Irwin (left) was a Delta farmer and MLA who had dreams of leading the Socreds. He managed to get only one vote to Bennett's fourteen when the newly elected caucus chose its leader and premier. Irwin settled for the position of House Speaker instead, and he had his hands full keeping order when the Sommers storm broke.

On February 15 he was again on his feet. This time he took careful aim with a more damaging punch: "I firmly believe that money talks and has talked. We must find out what is going on in this Bennett-Gunderson government or the rest of us are wasting our time. Those two are selling you down the river and I mean that." Gibson deliberately targeted Bennett and his top advisor. Sommers' name was not mentioned, and he watched the exchange quietly.

Then pandemonium, never far from the surface in this B.C. legislature, erupted with shouting and yelling. Gibson charged that there was "barefaced misrepresentation and unfairness" in the Squamish dispute. A tight-lipped Bennett shouted, "Be careful." But the Bull was not to be stopped. "I don't believe no money passed. Somebody passed something to somebody," he contended. Hardly a specific charge, but reporters rushed to the phones with the fiery allegations.

Gibson demanded the licence question be placed before the House Forestry Committee and charged Bennett was afraid to do so. Flushed and furious, Bennett ignored the taunts, leaving the House as Gibson shouted, "I don't wonder that Mr. Premier walks out. He can't take it." Gibson refused to let go. He said he didn't know how licences were approved, but he was sure that money talked.

The government sloughed off Gibson's charges, referring to them as more rantings from the Bull of the Woods, but the Socreds misjudged the seriousness of the accusations and the impression the charges would leave with the public. In fact, they triggered the government's first major crisis, raising a question of honesty that tore at the Socreds' credibility for the remainder of Bennett's twenty-year reign. Damning newspaper coverage the next day made clear the damage, a deep stain on Bennett's hitherto pure image. The House was tense as Bonner read from clippings and then demanded that Gibson withdraw "implications of false motives." Gibson refused and Speaker Tom Irwin ordered him out until the House decided what to do.

Gibson stormed from the chamber to the applause of his colleagues. In a scene that might have come from a comic opera, he dashed up the stairs and took a seat in the public gallery. A government member immediately shouted, "There is a stranger in the House," an ancient parliamentary cry. This centuries-old tradition refers to the presence of an outsider or opponent who has no right to hear or be party to a debate. It is a move guaranteed to bring the business of the House to a halt.

Gibson responded in a booming voice from above, "I'm either a member on the floor of the House, or a private citizen up here in the gallery." He ignored two confused guards standing nearby. There was much argument and debate on the floor about what to do next, as Gibson was the first MLA ever ordered out of the B.C. legislature.

A CCF member compared what Gibson had said to a comment made much earlier by old-timer Tom Uphill, a veteran of many riotous scenes in the House. At the height of the Gibson furor, the opposing member cited Uphill's comment, "From what you heard they are the biggest bunch of crooks that ever sat on that side of the House." The Socreds were too smart, however, to suggest Tom be evicted. Trying to throw out this veteran of the B.C. legislature for his previous unparliamentary comments would have caused them even more grief.

Speaker Tom Irwin later sent Gibson a note saying he could return to the House while the matter was under consideration. The unrepentant Gibson told reporters, "Bennett obviously told his puppets to keep their mouths buttoned."

The government realized it was in trouble and tried some damage control. Later the next day Attorney General Bonner rose to his feet in the House to announce a decision made only a few hours earlier by cabinet. Obviously shaken by the accusations, the government appointed Mr. Justice Arthur Lord as a one-man commission to probe Gibson's charges. Gibson happily bellowed, "Victory."

Crowds that had packed the public galleries to view a continuation of the ruckus were sadly disappointed when it came to such a tame ending. Gaglardi, however, couldn't resist a final jab at his sparring partner, "The bigger they are the harder they fall," he yelled over at Gibson, who observed that at least the diminutive Gaglardi "didn't have too far to fall."

Bennett later downplayed the appointment of the commission to reporters, stating it would not be much of an inquiry but was created simply "because we just want to let the sunshine in." Judge Lord confirmed that the call to head up the commission had been very sudden and he wouldn't go ahead until "the government tells us how deep it wants to go." He told the press that the probe would be "pretty wide open." It wasn't, nor was it deep or penetrating, and it only let in a feeble ray of sunshine.

The *Vancouver Sun* editorialized that the government had "done the right thing" by setting up the commission, while the *Province* said it had "retrieved a bad blunder" and that Gibson should have been challenged as soon as he made the accusations.

What was not known at the time was the consternation created in the offices of Wick Gray and Charlie Schultz when the Lord commission was announced. The transactions in which money passed from Schultz to Gray to Sommers had occurred quietly, often with no documentation. Gray made a hurried trip to Victoria and asked Sommers to sign notes for the amounts received. Gray said his accountant, Charles Eversfield, had heard rumours about bribes. Eversfield, he said, was a nervous man who had become aware that some of the transactions between Schultz, Gray, and Sommers were not properly documented. The accountant, Gray explained, was anxious to keep himself free of a charge of complicity if the dealings became public knowledge. He wanted everything documented properly. At the same time, Charlie Schultz sent several files home with his secretary for temporary safekeeping.

The Lord Commission

As tenacious as his name suggested, prominent lawyer Alfred Bull was the counsel for the commission when Mr. Justice Lord opened his hearing into Gibson's charges on March 7, 1955. The lawyer representing Gibson was W.T. Brown.

Only one witness was called, a man who could have blown the issue wide open, but didn't because he was afraid of losing his job. Dr. Chauncy D. Orchard was B.C.'s chief forester and deputy minister of the department. He was hesitant and nervous in the witness box and said only that he knew of no dishonesty in the granting of FMLs. He explained how some aspects of the licence system worked. The holder of a licence paid a stumpage fee to the government of $2.54 per thousand board feet, compared to the average $6.72 paid by small independent loggers. The holder of a licence was required, however, to build his own roads, provide forest protection in case of fire, and to hire qualified personnel to survey and manage the area. The government's forest service provided these services for small loggers. Orchard maintained the forest service was looking after small loggers better than before and said working circles were maintained for those who wanted to log but did not have the expertise or the personnel to take on responsibility for developing and maintaining the licence areas. One of the problems with the old system had been that the small logger, often short of funds and operating with old equipment or inexperienced personnel, left a harvested area in poor shape, subject to erosion or difficult to reforest.

The chief forester told the hearing that twenty FMLs had been issued since 1948, seven by the Socreds and the rest by the former Coalition government. He said three other applications, including BCFP's, had been turned down for various inadequacies, and 29 hopefuls had more recently been told they could start to prepare submissions. The first step, he said, was for companies to notify the public of their intentions through newspaper advertisements, which would allow those opposed to an application to prepare their counter-arguments.

Years after his retirement, Dr. Orchard related what he had not disclosed to the Lord commission. He said his forest department officials had raised serious objections to the first BCFP application, and so he had refused to approve it. He described an angry meeting with Sommers early in 1955, when he was asked for a written statement of approval for FML #22, BCFP's second application. His

meeting with the forests minister followed E.P. Taylor's visit to the
Empress Hotel for discussions with Bennett, Sommers, and Gunderson.
Orchard said he adamantly refused to approve the application. He
said Sommers insisted the premier had indicated Orchard favoured
the application. The chief forester maintained he told Sommers that
if this was the case, the premier was an unqualified liar. He asked to
see Bennett, but Sommers refused to arrange a meeting. Orchard said
he told Sommers he would have nothing to do with "doctoring" the
closed file. In later years Orchard referred to his old boss as "the
infamous, treacherous R.E. Sommers."

At the Lord hearing, Gibson's lawyer, W.T. Brown, refused to put
his client on the stand, contending that because Gibson had been
thrown out of the House and referred to as "a stranger in the House,"
he might have lost his parliamentary immunity and be liable to slander
suits. Brown told the hearing that Gibson had not pointed the finger
at any one person, but had alluded to how the big, wealthy operator
was favoured by the system over the small logger. He certainly hadn't
named Sommers, but few who followed events in the House doubted
he meant the minister of lands and forests.

After three days the Lord commission, which cost $2,000, wound
up with the commissioner finding there had been "no improprieties."
Without Gibson's booming accusations, there was no case to be made.
Gibson said later he had wanted to go on the stand, but his lawyer
vetoed the idea. "Not one-tenth of the evidence I wanted to bring out
was brought out," Gibson stated. He was left wide open to his
opponents' eager accusations that he was a deflated windbag. Bennett
chortled, "I said the Liberal Party was going down the drain. The plug
was pulled on them this morning."

The old Bull was wounded, but he was far from through. He felt the
judge had dismissed his whole argument, and the Socreds now had
ammunition with which to silence him and bury the issue. To keep his
accusations alive he announced he would resign his seat in the legislature
and take his battle to the subsequent by-election, which he would contest.
He was determined to continue challenging the Socreds' handling of the
forest licence issue and to support the small logger. Gibson went
confidently into the fray because he believed he had persuaded the CCF
and the Conservatives not to run candidates in the by-election, thus
leaving the way open for a direct face-off between himself and Bennett's
as-yet unnamed Socred candidate. Much would happen, however,
between March and the September shootout at Lillooet.

H.R. MacMillan (left) and C.D. Orchard did not often see eye to eye on forestry matters, but they both had respect for former chief forester E.C. Manning and attended the opening of the park named in his honour. A New Brunswick native, Orchard came to B.C. in 1920 and started work with the forest service, where he remained for the rest of his career. In 1941 he became chief forester and deputy minister of forests when his predecessor, Manning, was killed in an airplane crash.

Sloan Takes Another Look

Two weeks before Judge Lord began his hearing into Gibson's charges, another commission opened that would have a far-reaching effect on both the future of the forest industry and the fate of Forests Minister Bob Sommers. The Lord commission, the second Sloan commission, and the criminal trial that followed were all intertwined like the roots of a gnarled old tree.

In 1944, Mr. Justice Gordon Sloan had been appointed by the Coalition government to conduct an intensive investigation into "apprehensions, complaints and regulatory problems plaguing the forest industry." His report in 1948 recommended the introduction of the controversial FML system. Eleven years to the day from the start of his first inquiry, on February 21, 1955, Mr. Justice Sloan opened a second hearing into the industry. He was brought back because Premier Bennett recognized the complaints that had triggered the original 1944 commission were resurfacing in Gibson's allegations and because Bennett had great respect for Sloan's abilities as a judge and arbitrator.

Gordon Sloan was 59 years of age, a native of Nanaimo and a World War I flyer who had been a member of the provincial bar since 1921. He had been attorney general in Pattullo's Liberal government from 1933 until he resigned in 1937. Sloan had headed his first commission in 1940 and had had considerable experience since then leading inquiries and probes into health, fisheries, railways, and workers' compensation. In this instance he was an obvious choice for the job, having headed the previous forest inquiry.

A clash of political and industry views about the management of B.C. forests echoed throughout the testimony presented to this Sloan commission, fostering a growing public awareness that all was not right in the woods. This atmosphere played into Gibson's hands as he continued his unrelenting crusade against Sommers and the system. While Bennett had not yet set the date for the Lillooet by-election, the Sloan hearings provided a platform and an audience for Gibson's comeback campaign. In May 1955, the man who would run again for a seat in Lillooet appeared at the inquiry and faced a battery of lawyers representing the province's largest and most influential companies. Chief among them were BCFP attorneys Cecil Merritt, F. Craig Monroe, and Walter Owen.

Gordon Gibson maintained the forest industry was controlled through "hotel room deals." (Lawyers did not ask him to identify what deals he meant, but as an opposition politician he must have heard rumours of the Empress Hotel meeting attended by Bennett, Sommers, E.P. Taylor, Hector Munro, and others, which resulted in FML #22 being awarded to BCFP.)

Lawyer Cecil Merritt asked Gibson if he was suggesting that Sommers was open to bribery. "Nothing of the kind," said Gibson evasively. He claimed he was simply criticizing the system and that he had always maintained B.C. needed an independent forest commission with the power to make timber-cutting allocations, free of government interference and politics. Gibson was quietly pleased, however, that Merritt had linked Sommers' name with bribery in the question.

He brought up the suggestion of bribery again when he was asked to explain his concerns about logging in the Squamish area. He charged that BCFP had bought off a Squamish logger, Sammy Craig, by

Gordon Sloan had ties to the Liberal Party, but Bennett trusted his knowledge of the forest industry and his even-handed approach to justice. Sloan headed a 1944 royal commission of inquiry into the forest industry, which brought down a report in 1948 that was destined to change forest tenure in B.C. forever. In 1955 Bennett named Sloan to head a second royal commission to take another look at the state of the industry and put to rest rumours that "money talked."

promising to give him 26 million board feet of timber for his mill from one of its working-circle allocations. (FML #22 included a small section of land in the Squamish district.) Gibson said as soon as Craig was offered the deal, he threw away a 100-name petition against the BCFP application that he had canvassed in his community.

During his testimony, Gibson claimed the public was being bamboozled by a much-touted requirement of FMLs that forest roads be made available for public use as well as for the industry's logging trucks. He said that in its resubmitted application, BCFP had promised to build roads "as a sort of payoff. They are building it because they are getting the forest licence. It isn't kindness coming out of their heart." Gibson maintained that roads for the public should never be part of forest policy. Gibson ended this diatribe by asking F. Craig Monroe how it was that C.D. Schultz and Associates was now handling all forest company licence applications.

Monroe claimed it was a "diabolical lie" to suggest Schultz's company had influence in the government's granting of FMLs. He raised the question of the Gibson family holding a licence to operate Vancouver radio station CKLG. Monroe argued that if FMLs represented a power grab, so did the granting of a radio licence.

Monroe's suggestion that there could be anything improper in the granting of a licence for CKLG raised Gibson's ire. He bellowed back at Monroe, "It is said around town that you are a good one to see if you want a forest management licence. I think you would be wise to keep away from my personal life." Gibson was alluding to the lawyer's reputed role in smoothing the way for licence applicants through his representations for C.D. Schultz and Associates. Monroe complained that Gibson had taken the opportunity "to make a vicious attack on me" and explained he had simply been retained by Charlie Schultz to advise companies making applications.

This argument raged back and forth for some time, Gibson using every opportunity to further his election campaign. He was for the little guy, he said, and the Socreds and Sommers were giving everything away to the big guys.

Gibson told the commission that the price of BCFP stock had increased in value by a total of $6 million after its application was approved. He argued that the current FML system created windfall profits for shareholders the minute they were awarded, and decisions were being made by people in government who knew nothing about the economics of the industry.

In addition to his testimony at the inquiry, Gibson was delivering his message at public meetings and to any reporter who would listen. One of the BCFP lawyers, Walter Owen, took a swing at Gibson without naming him. Owen complained to Sloan, "There appears to be a deliberate campaign by some person to arouse public prejudice against the large companies in the forest industry." The lawyer resented his clients being labelled "wrongdoers," and contended, "It is an insidious underhanded attempt to blacken the reputation of honorable men before they have a chance to speak for themselves."

All this exchange was a bonus for Gibson, as it reflected badly on the large companies. His case was further bolstered by men like logging operator Arthur Benedickson, who told Sloan, "Under the free enterprise system we have had—we are going to run out of timber some time."

During the sessions, several of the small operators and others expressed serious concerns about overcutting and inadequate reforestation of the coastal forest. There were also charges that too much valuable timber was locked up in parks, where it was being left to die and rot when it could be salvaged and sold.

H.G. Williams, a government forester, made an early case against large clearcuts on the coast, suggesting that smaller ones were less damaging to interdependent ecosystems. He explained that the Douglas fir, the most valuable coastal tree, tended to re-seed itself more readily over an area up to a quarter mile from the tree, and therefore no logging strip should be more than a half mile wide.

As the Sloan commission continued its hearings, E.P. Taylor got what he wanted. The forests minister announced the approval of FML #22, granted to BCFP effective May 18, 1955, overriding the objections of his deputy minister, C.D. Orchard. The agreement was signed by R.E. Sommers and H.G. Munro. It covered an area of central Vancouver Island amounting to 193,695 acres and was also known as the "Maquinna Forest Management Licence." The terms included requirements that BCFP would provide new roads into Port Renfrew and the Kennedy Lake area and would construct a new pulp and/or paper mill to be completed and operating at full capacity by September 1, 1959. There were also accommodations for working circles in the area, as the licence stated "The provision for competitive bidding for logging in blocks four and five is to become effective not later than January 1, 1960."

When he awarded the licence, Sommers stated it was "one of the most far-sighted and significant, as far as the welfare of British Columbians are concerned, since the licensing procedure was established." Speaking in Victoria, the minister maintained that the roadbuilding provisions in the licence meant that for the first time there would be public access to the west coast of Vancouver Island. He said that BCFP would spend an extra $750,000 to take the road to the coast. He was carried away by his own enthusiasm when he suggested that new hunting, fishing, and beach recreational areas would surpass some in Hawaii and Florida.

The opponents battled to the end. Gibson even borrowed some rhetoric from Winston Churchill when he told the media, "Never in history have so few men who know so little given away so much of the property of so many others." The FML gave BCFP the forest reserves it needed to expand and immediately increased its share price from $9 to $13.50. An outraged Gibson contended this was a shareholders' profit gained at the expense of working circle operators. Robert Bonner claimed critics were "narrow and selfish" and the move was in the best interests of the people of B.C. All of it was political rhetoric.

(By the early 1960s E.P. Taylor had increased BCFP's holdings to include eight logging operations on Vancouver Island and three on the mainland. There were two sawmills at Victoria, one at Youbou, one on Cowichan Lake, and one at Hammond, as well as a plywood mill in Victoria. The company held licences to harvest timber in an area covering 478,000 acres in the Vancouver forest district and another 185,000 acres on the B.C. mainland. In 1961, two years later than promised, the pulp mill built under the terms of FML #22 was added to the company's assets. BCFP also made Vancouver history in 1960 when the city's first five-alarm fire tore through the spruce division at False Creek, causing $2 million damage.)

Premier Bennett sailed off to Hawaii for a holiday in June, believing the decision to establish a second Sloan commission had temporarily stamped out the political fire and Gibson's allegations about FMLs. The Commission was still sitting, so Bennett knew he could stall criticism by stating simply that the question was under review and could not be discussed. He also anticipated it would be some time before Sloan came in with his report. He knew without doubt by this time that there was going to be trouble with Sommers, but he did not foresee the intensity of heat that would develop in the coming firestorm.

However, as long as the economy kept pumping money into the treasury, Bennett could do no wrong in the eyes of his supporters, and there were ample signs there was a lot more money on the way. Bennett's credo was that boom times, bulldozers, and blacktop would overcome, at least in the short term, any vague suspicion about payoffs, and up to this time the only charges had come from Gibson. They could be discounted as the posturing of a blustering, out-of-control, political opponent.

In the meantime, Bennett's dream was unfolding. Roadbuilding crews worked throughout the summer months, and construction began on the extension of the PGE Railway into North Vancouver. Dusty backroads, long ignored, were manicured into mini-autobahns. It all provided jobs, encouraged the purchase of local supplies and rental of large equipment owned by local firms, and it was guaranteed to pay off at the voting booth. "Flying Phil" Gaglardi could hardly keep up with announcements about the blizzard of new contracts being let by his highways department. The Socreds were on the move, and the opposition could only watch and wonder at Bennett's winning ways with voters.

While Sommers kept a low profile, Bennett enjoyed a giant July love-in at Port Alberni with the province's leading forest tycoon, H.R. MacMillan. It was the opening of a new $35 million pulp mill project, and every aspect, every statistic was sweet music to Socred ears.

Bennett pulled the lever that drove in the first of 7,000 pilings for a deep-sea dock to handle ships taking on loads for the growing export market. Up to 90 percent of the 300 tons of pulp to be produced daily was destined for overseas buyers. The project would create 600 construction jobs and 300 permanent ones. The *Province* newspaper cautioned that while the jobs were more than welcome, the small size of the permanent workforce compared to the scope of the operation pointed to the inroads automation was making on the industry.

H.R. told the crowd, "There is no more active father of free enterprise in the past three years than our premier who has given strong support to the extension of industrial enterprise." A beaming Bennett modestly noted that these were pleasant words "in these days when everyone is critical of everything." He paid tribute to H.R., who had "a vision of what could be accomplished by the proper use of our forests."

The economy continued to soar. Elk Falls Co. Ltd. announced a $13.5 million expansion at its Duncan Bay Mill, including the addition of a $7.5 million paper machine with a 50,000-ton annual capacity. Bennett was also on hand for a ceremony marking a $6 million plant expansion at Port Moody. On his home ground in Castlegar, Sommers announced construction of a $30 million, 300-ton-per-day pulp mill, with an initial 1,000 construction jobs. At the Harmac mill near Nanaimo, a $250,000 odour-control project was begun. The industry as a whole reported that its 1954 sales had hit record figures totalling $528 million, $16 million more than the year earlier.

The International Woodworkers of America, with some 30,000 members in B.C., signed a two-year contract for a five-cent-an-hour pay hike and improved fringe benefits. It meant peace in the woods for at least two years.

Everything was coming up roses for the Socreds as the premier set the date for the crucial Lillooet by-election on which Gibson had staked his political future and the success of his crusade. For Bennett and the Bull, everything would be decided on September 12.

Blitzkrieg

The by-election blitzkrieg planned by the premier during the summer of 1955 was aimed at blowing Gibson away for good, but the opening salvos fizzled. Beginning in June, B.C. was caught up in a royal commission investigating the Vancouver police department that took

Phil Gaglardi was probably Bennett's most controversial minister, in charge of public works and then highways from 1952 till 1968. For years there were newsmaking allegations of favours and graft in roadbuilding contracts, as well as stories of his speeding on highways when he headed home to Kamloops for the weekend. Photographer Jim Ryan took this shot in 1962 when Gaglardi had lost his driver's licence for three months after being charged with speeding and driving without due care and attention. In 1968 he resigned his portfolio in the midst of a scandal about misuse of a government jet, which he much preferred to his automobile.

media attention away from almost everything else. Chief Walter Mulligan was a top cop on the take, and the public was treated daily to new revelations and scandals. Stories of Mulligan and his men filled the front pages of all the newspapers and shoved politics to second billing.

Bennett got one headline he didn't want. It tied his Vernon hardware store to a government project. Furious at the jibes of his opponents, W.A.C. gave written instructions to the provincial comptroller general and all purchasing agents that they were not to do any kind of direct business with Bennett Hardware. He explained that the $6,000 in purchases referred to in the story were made by the primary contractor and there was nothing wrong with Bennett's store sub-contracting. It was a fine point, but the issue died.

When the Lillooet campaign finally moved into high gear, bulldozers, trucks, cranes, and everything mechanical that could be mustered rolled into the riding like an invading force. Roadbuilding and public construction, the politicians' aces, were always conspicuous winners during Bennett's election battles.

The CCF and Conservative riding associations ignored suggestions that they not contest the by-election. In a four-way fight including the Liberals, Socreds, Conservatives, and CCF, Gibson was doomed. The other three candidates all lived in the riding; it was no help that he lived in Vancouver. The slumping popularity of his provincial leader, Art Laing, was also a hindrance, and it must have hurt the Liberal-loving *Victoria Times* to publish a poll that said 80 percent of those polled felt the Liberals didn't know what they were talking about. The Socreds got the approval of 49 percent. The other parties were nowhere. How accurate it was didn't matter, but it was a portent of things to come.

The Social Credit candidate, Don Robinson, was a young railway engineer with the PGE—not Bennett's choice but a well-known local man. Socred cabinet ministers poured into Lillooet, making promises and announcing giveaways. Surrounding districts were denuded of trucks and equipment to beef up the blitz. Bob Bonner said that in three years the Socreds had built more than a third of the province's 20,000 miles of highways, while Gaglardi predicted the Lillooet district would benefit greatly from even more roads.

Sommers announced that a local application for an FML licence had been put on hold during the campaign. Gibson hit back, contending Sommers already had given away hundreds of millions of dollars in forest licences. "He knows this is wrong. He knows this is not right," he told voters.

Meetings in small communities throughout the Lillooet district provided never-before-seen entertainment as the Socreds and Gibson laid into each other in jam-packed halls. The debate was punctuated by many threats of "a punch on the nose," as supporters of the two camps clashed. "Stormiest in Years" was one headline as papers reported the charges of bribery and lying that were hurled back and forth by all parties during feverish smear campaigns.

At another meeting Bennett bellowed, "You are a traitor to the Social Credit movement" when he saw a former constituency president who quit over the FML issue. Bennett still relied on Sommers' competence and superior ability on a platform and often joined him

Art Laing (left) and Arnold Webster became the leaders of the Liberals and the CCF respectively before the 1953 election. Laing left Ottawa to improve his party's standing in B.C., but failed in the attempt and returned to the federal governments of Lester Pearson and later Pierre Trudeau.

Arnold Webster was a school principal before becoming CCF leader. Quiet, moderate, and from the Christian wing of the party, he had no better luck than his predecessor, Harold Winch, at gaining power. He was leader only until 1956.

at meetings. He later commented, "Sommers was a great campaigner—a great schoolteacher. He'd take a blackboard and pointer and he'd show the problems and analyze them."

If he couldn't move heaven, Bennett certainly could move earth. When a half-dozen householders in the tiny community of Britannia Beach on Howe Sound complained that the new PGE track would block their view, Bennett saw some gain at little cost. Ever the populist, he responded, "We will see that those houses are raised up and a full basement placed under them." The cost, of course, would be borne by the PGE.

It was hardly surprising that Bennett was exultant when the votes were counted. The sword had been thrust through the heart of the Bull. The final tally was Social Credit, 1,709; Liberal, 1,279; CCF, 944; and Progressive Conservative, 201. The House now stood at 28 Socreds, 14 CCF, 4 Liberals, and 2 Independents. (Between the 1953 election and the Lillooet by-election, the Socreds had lost a by-election to the Liberals. Now their majority returned to its 1953 numbers.)

In post-election statements, switching from the low road to the high road, Bennett told reporters piously, "The people want their affairs conducted in a dignified manner and they resent political smears and unwarranted attacks on men in public life." Sommers chipped in that it was "a great victory for our movement." He took comfort from the fact that his own predicament had been a low-key issue.

Once more it was never-say-die time for Gibson as he talked to the press. He stated that defeat would give him more time to thrash away on his issues. "I don't think the people as a whole gripped the importance of the basic issue of forest management. I was working for the people and Bennett was working for himself and his political machine," said Gibson, repeating that he was far from through.

The *Province* editorialized, "Mr. Bennett earned his victory." He gave his opponents "the works—public works!" The paper said, "[The premier] has behind him a live, hardworking, devoted organization." The other parties were "strife-torn," and "Mr. B. can grin to some purpose."

For the victor, Mr. Robinson, it was time for probably the most profound remark in his undistinguished political career. He declared that Rome wasn't built in a day, but "it would have been if Bennett had been running things."

H.R. MacMillan

When H.R. MacMillan spoke about B.C. forests, everyone listened. Politicians, the public, the industry, the unions, all stopped what they were doing to take in the words of the revered, sometimes feared, old tycoon. He was big in business, but also big physically, and unlike Gordon Gibson he was a cultured old smoothie, a university graduate, and a self-proclaimed self-made man. Admired throughout the community, he lived graciously and at 70 still had an armlock on the industry.

MacMillan was a personal friend of E.P. Taylor, the man who had persuaded Taylor to invest in B.C.'s forest industry. MacMillan's company managed BCFP during its formative years and then recommended Hector Munro as the company's first president.

In November 1955, H.R. appeared before the Sloan commission with a massive 50,000-word brief that traced the history of B.C.'s lumber industry from its beginnings. His staff maintained that much of the work and the writing was his own. He rattled the industry by telling Sloan that no more licences should be issued in the Vancouver Forest District—a sweeping area that at that time contained much of southwestern B.C. from the coast to the Cascade Mountains and from

H.R. MacMillan grew up in Ontario, raised by his widowed mother and his grandparents. He studied biology and forestry (and was described as one of the most brilliant forestry students ever to attend Yale) and joined the Canadian forest service in 1909. By 1912 he was B.C.'s first chief forester. This sketch of MacMillan was retrieved from B.C. Forest Service records. In the 1920s H.R. left the public service to set up his own lumber export company, which eventually became MacMillan Bloedel Ltd.

the Queen Charlotte Islands down to the U.S. border—and especially not on Vancouver Island. MacMillan warned of massive overcutting in the region. "Every overcut, particularly of Douglas fir, heads us onto the edge of the precipice," declared the man who was B.C.'s first chief forester before he built his own empire. H.R. said the Douglas fir overcut was 117 percent and it represented 39 percent of all trees cut in 1954.

Although he was an opponent of FMLs when Sloan first proposed them, believing they would cost his company a great deal of money, MacMillan said that he had changed his view, explaining, "I was only 60 then. I am ready to admit I have changed my mind on many things as I have gotten older," he added, drawing chuckles from the crowd. He no longer saw FMLs as giveaways, but believed they were necessary for proper forest management and the extension of the sustained yield policy.

Still, he also strongly supported the little guy. "For whosoever hath, to him shall be given and he shall have more abundance; but whosoever hath not, from him shall be taken away even that which he hath," he said, turning biblical to describe how the companies with money could afford to buy more timber while the cash-strapped independent loggers were shut out of FMLs. "Small loggers should not be in the position of sharecroppers," he said, calling for the creation of more working circles with dedicated sources of trees for small operators. To promote this he urged construction of more roads into Crown lands.

MacMillan contended that "small sawmills should be kept alive as long as possible by holding all Crown land Douglas fir for their use." MacMillan also argued that the export of unmanufactured wood from B.C. was contrary to the public interest.

The *Sun* editorialized that it was strange to hear a monopolist speak for the little guy, running a headline that said, "Forest Democracy Gets Boost from Mr. Big." It noted that even ten years after Sloan's initial report, B.C. was still in danger of producing itself out of its greatest provincial resource.

Other industry spokesmen hit out at H.R.'s suggestion of no more licences, claiming that he simply wanted to lock the gates after his multimillion-dollar interests were well secured. B.J. Kelley was head of the Forest Development Policy Association, a group of sixteen medium- to large-sized sawmill operators, three of whom had FMLs while the others had applications under consideration by Sommers. Kelley claimed mature timber would be wiped out in 75 years without the kind of management ensured by the FMLs. He maintained MacMillan had "either an overwhelming fear of socialism or a desire to stifle further competition in his operations on the Lower Mainland and Vancouver Island," by suggesting there be no more FMLs granted in the Vancouver district.

At the Sloan commission, Gordon Wismer was the lawyer representing the Policy Association. He was a flamboyant, controversial, former attorney general in the Coalition government, defeated when the Socred government rolled in. Wismer dubbed H.R. a "benevolent monarch" and maintained that when Sloan originally proposed the FML system, he did so because there was "fear in the minds of the public that four or five firms would take over," MacMillan's being one of them.

L.L. "Poldi" Bentley, vice-president of Canadian Forest Products Limited (later Canfor), accused MacMillan of trying to impose a "wooden curtain." He contended the MacMillan empire had the financial clout to move in and buy licences from independent loggers while at the same time profiting from the licences it already held.

Another key B.C. industrialist, Walter Koerner, president of Alaska Pine and Cellulose, also took a different tack from H.R. and maintained that there was an annual 1.5 million board feet of lumber *undercut* in the Vancouver district. He declared that projections for a 90-year replacement cycle for coastal trees were wrong. He said it was actually 52 to 59 years. Koerner urged proper management to ensure forest regeneration and said new policies were required to "ensure that the maximum contribution is made by the forests towards improving the general economic and social lives of B.C. people, this is the prime objective."

In a parting shot at the hearing, H.R. said government taxes threatened B.C.'s competitive position in global markets. Referring to the industry's $520 million business and the impact it had on the entire province, MacMillan warned, "B.C. has too many eggs in one basket, lumber." He said an expansion of pulp and paper production would give B.C.'s forest industry a better balance.

Judge Sloan's report did not appear until nearly two years after MacMillan's testimony, and he continued to hear submissions for several more months. In the meantime, small storm clouds that had been gathering around Sommers were turning into thunderheads, and in December a witness appeared before the commission who put the allegations of bribery back on the front pages. It was to be an unmerry Christmas for Bob.

Sturdy's Startling Revelations

More and more people were surfacing with stories about Sommers. One of Charlie Schultz's employees was prepared to sing for money. The individual told Gordon Gibson there were peculiar financial arrangements between Schultz, Wick Gray, and BCFP. Much as he wanted all he could get on Sommers, Gibson turned down the offer of information. He knew that money-tainted evidence could damage the case he was trying to build.

Charles Eversfield, however, was a different story. He was up to his neck in the dealings between Gray and Sommers and wanted all the help he could get to exculpate himself if and when any charges were laid. Eversfield had been Wick Gray's accountant for five years. He was 45 years old, slightly built, and balding. A family man, originally from the Fraser Valley, he claimed he had no particular political leanings, but in the fall of 1955, just before he left Canada for the United States, he visited the office of an old friend, David Sturdy, lawyer and long-time Liberal. Eversfield said he wanted to tell his story to someone he knew and trusted. The accountant told Sturdy that the situation had bothered him for some time and he was moving to the U.S., where he felt he might be able to avoid trouble and notoriety if the law stepped in.

Sturdy took the ticking political time bomb to Gibson, who consulted Liberal colleagues. Gibson decided to bankroll Sturdy for a trip to Los Angeles, where Eversfield was living, in order to obtain a sworn statement along with the accountant's copies of what Eversfield claimed were incriminating documents removed from Wick Gray's office.

The Liberals felt Eversfield's revelations were essential for the long-term battle against the Socreds and had immediate relevance for an upcoming Vancouver by-election scheduled for January. The Socreds were pinning their hopes on Les Peterson, a young lawyer some saw as the future leader of the party.

The incidents and decisions that followed had far-reaching ramifications in the unfolding political drama. In early December Bob Bonner received an anonymous phone call warning him that political opponents were set to unleash a forestry scandal. Bonner talked to Sommers, who said he knew nothing about it. On December 7, however, Sturdy requested a meeting with Bonner in the attorney general's office. The lawyer claimed he had close to 200 documents and Eversfield's signed statement, which indicated money talked in the issuance of FMLs. Bonner was unimpressed despite the alleged authenticity of the material. Sturdy demanded a full-blown royal commission to investigate the charges; Bonner offered a confidential police inquiry. The attorney general didn't disguise his hostility, almost certain that this was a political set-up linked to the upcoming by-election. The meeting ended in stalemate.

Sommers later said that after Bonner reported to Bennett, the attorney general called him in. Sommers finally admitted he had borrowed $7,000 from Wick Gray and later signed notes for the money. Bonner told Sommers to redeem them immediately because "the situation might be misunderstood if it became public knowledge." Sommers took out an $8,000 bank loan and paid Gray $7,100. He now realized the dangers if his convoluted financial dealings became public knowledge.

Bonner wired David Sturdy the next day, "Had no prior knowledge of purpose of your visit yesterday but anonymous phone call to expect attack upon a government minister made sense by the time you left. Your mysterious behaviour, including refusal to discuss subject matter of interview in arranging appointment, desire to conceal whereabouts of your informant, your advice that informant had in hand all sorts of material, supposedly purporting allegations made for two years but not presented to Lord Commission and that you are advised of such material as long ago as September, together with contents of today's wire, all now coinciding with a by-election campaign, fills me with a profound skepticism towards the entire matter, particularly in view of the minister's reactions. In the circumstances, your unsupported document and your suggestion of criminal conspiracy or activity by the directors and management of seven companies seems far-fetched."

Sturdy wired back the next day, stating that the answer was totally unsatisfactory and he planned further action. Realizing it was far from a bluff, Bonner replied, suggesting another meeting the following week, but Sturdy labelled this simply stalling and said he wasn't prepared to accept some vague date.

A week later, on December 16, Sturdy appeared before the Sloan commission. He said he possessed a "certain body of evidence that, if proved true, could form the basis for an inference that the Minister of Lands and Forests had received considerations for the issuance of forest management licences." Sloan refused to hear Sturdy's complaint, stating it was not within the purview of his commission.

Reporters now had what they needed, however, and they dashed for the phones. Here was the first public statement linking Sommers to Gibson's money-talks accusation of almost a year earlier. After months of baiting and abuse, the Bull had gored his opponents and drawn blood. Sturdy told reporters he was acting strictly as a private citizen, although obviously a Liberal private citizen. In Victoria, Sommers came out of a cabinet meeting and was confronted by the press. Visibly shaken by the questioning, he stated, "It is certainly not true. I cannot understand it." When approached for comment, an angry Bennett asked reporters what Sommers had said. When told, Bennett barked, "Well then that's it," and took off down the hall.

A few days later, Sommers made a legal move that was to stall the affair for almost two years. Lawyer George Hauser appeared in a Vancouver court and filed a libel suit on Sommers' behalf against David Sturdy "for damages for the publication of a libel contained in a statutory declaration purposed to have been made by Charles W. Eversfield" and presented by Sturdy to the Sloan commission. The action sought damages for slander. This manoeuvre effectively blocked the possibility of any criminal charges being laid until it was resolved. Sommers told reporters that the sole reason for the suit was to clear his name.

David Sturdy said he would immediately prepare a defence against the charge. He told reporters he had asked Bonner to enlarge the scope of the Sloan commission or to order an independent investigation. "I am not saying the evidence is true, but I want it investigated. I am going to do something about this, somehow, somewhere, sometime," Sturdy stated emphatically. Sometime was, however, a long time coming. Early indications were that the libel case might go to trial in a couple of months, but that wasn't the way Sommers, his advisors, and the government wanted it.

The libel case was to haunt Bonner for the next two years and cause a split in Socred ranks. Some backbenchers such as Cyril Shelford, Irvine Corbett, and Fred Sharp, who were not in on cabinet discussions, saw it as nothing but a delaying tactic that would postpone the resolution of the broader issue. They were concerned about the damage being done to the image of the party as well as to themselves and Sommers' wife and children. The move did, however, keep the lid on the crisis, and without question the suit served the Socred political purpose. For almost two years Bennett was able to slough off all allegations, attacks, and charges from the opposition and the media by maintaining that nothing had been established legally, no charges laid, and nobody convicted.

Sommers Under Siege

Sommers was noticeably absent when the Socreds began the campaign to win the Vancouver Centre by-election. Bennett promised Vancouver another $1 million a year for civic improvement, and visions of new bridges danced in everyone's head. Improvements to the graceful but hopelessly inadequate Lions Gate Bridge, which spans the First Narrows of Burrard Inlet from Stanley Park to the North Shore, were also promised. The same promise has been made by successive governments for almost half a century.

Six cabinet ministers flanked Bennett in a rally that drew a crowd of 2,000 to the Georgia Auditorium. Sommers' problems were never mentioned, although Bennett made an oblique appeal to voters. "I ask you not to throw any sand in the gears. Some people want to stop the machinery, stop employment, stop industry." As the crowd roared its approval, Bennett said Ottawa was afraid that if people knew what Social Credit was achieving in B.C., the movement would sweep across the country.

Meanwhile, the Liberals were in trouble. Jack Gibson, Gordon's brother and a former MP, resigned as treasurer of the provincial party because of a decision by the party executive not to run a candidate in the by-election. One source said the Liberals felt they needed to get rid of some unpopular policies first, but the infighting and the decision not to compete in the race were heavy blows to both the Gibsons. Leader Art Laing came up with the excuse that because a general election was expected in the spring, the party had decided to sit out the by-election and keep its strength for the main bout. His assertion sounded more like a death rattle than a strategy.

The day before the by-election, Bennett held a press conference. James K. Nesbitt, *Sun* columnist in Victoria, noted, "It was all very whimsical and entertaining, educational and informative. The premier was in good form and looking well, and yes, there's no doubt that he's turning himself into a very gracious personality as well as one of the slickest politicians we have ever seen."

Bennett had every reason to be happy; he knew the by-election would be no contest. At the polls, Socred Les Peterson received more than 6,000 votes and was an easy winner.

Spirits were riding high despite the cloud that still hung over Sommers when the 1956 session opened in Victoria. An uproar was triggered early in the session when opposition members tried to ask about David Sturdy's charges against Sommers. Speaker Tom Irwin ruled there could be no reference to the charges while the case was before the courts, the ever-effective libel-action stonewall. Sommers sat silent and grim as the opposition called for his head. An angry Bennett jumped in, insisting that the court case prevented Bonner from making a statement.

The opposition wasn't buying it. The CCF's Bob Strachan pointed out there had been two months to say something before the suit was launched. Bonner stuck to his guns, maintaining there was "no body of evidence" to justify a royal commission or criminal charges. "This is the principle I hold and one which I will prevail on, whether or not it appears to be unpopular with the opposition," added the attorney general.

Art Laing accused Bennett of abdication of responsibility and said Bonner's wire to lawyer Sturdy was disgraceful. Bennett laughed and retorted, "It was a good wire." The row raged on, opposition members demanding Sommers drop his suit so a royal commission could be called. Legal manoeuvring should not obstruct justice they said. It was wasted effort. Bennett wasn't budging as the business of the House moved forward.

Bennett's February budget was a basket full of goodies. It was, at $258.5 million, the biggest spending spree in provincial history, three

Les Peterson was an easy winner in a 1956 by-election. He became minister of education and labour, and then minister of labour and attorney general, and was one of the ministers Bennett most trusted and relied upon. There was speculation that Peterson would succeed Bennett as Socred leader and premier, speculation fuelled by Bennett himself, but Peterson's ill-health and Bennett's longevity denied him this post.

times what it had been ten years earlier. Once again he played to the little guy and the rural voter. Bennett boosted the old-age pension supplement to $20 from $15, cut the entertainment tax from 15 percent to 10 percent, and hiked agricultural spending and grants to municipalities by a whopping 45 percent. The education budget was increased by $4 million, hospitals got an additional $1.5 million, and public servants received a 5 percent wage hike. The biggest outlay, however, was for highway construction and public works, a total of $80 million, most of it earmarked for roads outside the Lower Mainland. Critics maintained that it was a pre-election budget package, although voters had gone to the polls only three years earlier.

The budget was upbeat, but Sommers' problems still dogged Bennett in the legislature, and the intermingling of those problems, forest issues, politics, and government policy was once again evident in a confident, assertive speech that Sommers made in the legislature. He warned that some communities in the Douglas fir belt were facing disaster because of overcutting. He said it could be the death knell for some of the 20,000 loggers employed in the eastern part of the Vancouver Forest District. Sommers maintained the government's plans to cut fewer trees on a sustained yield basis could cost 4,000 logging jobs in the near future, but added that without these cuts now, in 25 years all 20,000 jobs would be gone. He contended only 20 percent of the area was being replanted and that a long-term tenure policy would give a large number of small and medium-sized operators a guaranteed supply of trees.

Sommers told legislators his remarks were not intended to

The 1956 legislative session was riotous but opened with the usual pomp and ceremony, Lieutenant Governor Frank Ross taking the salute on the steps of the legislature. He was accompanied by his wife, the mother of John Turner, who was to become a short term Canadian Prime Minister.

influence the Sloan commission, although it is difficult to imagine what other objective he could have had in mind. Without naming him, Sommers took a swing at archenemy Gibson. "It is time all members of the forest industry in B.C. developed a realistic sense of their responsibility to the people of the province," Sommers declared. He repeated his defence of FMLs, adding, however, they should be subject to performance reviews. Sommers pointed out that some opponents of the FML system were actually "free-booters," falsely touting the cause of free enterprise. He maintained that they were opposed to government intervention in the industry, preferring the old freewheeling style, which he had indicated was disaster bound. He left no doubt that the "free-booters" included Gibson.

Some forest industry leaders supported Sommers, others didn't. Poldi Bentley, at the time president of the B.C. Manufacturers Association, said he felt the minister was being unnecessarily gloomy, but Gordon Draeseke, secretary of Alaska Pine and Cellulose Ltd., agreed with the minister. Joe Morris, president of B.C. District of the

International Woodworkers of America, declared "misdirected policies" were responsible for trouble in the forests that could affect 60,000 jobs. He maintained that a loss of employment was not a necessary condition for sustained yield.

It didn't matter too much what Sommers said in the House when the Sloan commission hearings finally gave reporters and the public their first knowledge of Sommers' tea party with Argus boss E.P. Taylor in the fall of 1954. BCFP president Hector Munro was on the stand when lawyer Ronald Howard, representing the Western Forest Management Association, asked about the meeting. Munro said that when he learned Sommers was going east for his daughter's wedding in Detroit, he felt it would be good for the minister to meet Taylor and Argus Corporation directors. He added that he had business dealings with Wick Gray in 1953, but insisted BCFP didn't pay $2,500 to Gray for Sommers' expenses on the Toronto trip in 1954. Mr. Justice Sloan intervened and said this issue did not concern him.

Then, quite suddenly it seemed, newspapers reported that the Royal Canadian Mounted Police were investigating David Sturdy's allegations. When questioned by reporters, Bonner snapped, "When you can show me the basis of the reports I will comment." The papers stated that Liberal MLA George Gregory, who was acting as Sturdy's lawyer, had turned over material to RCMP Inspector W.J. Butler. Liberal MLA Bruce Brown told the legislature that the province now had the sorry spectacle of the chief law-enforcement officer asking police to investigate a brother cabinet minister. As Brown raked the government, Bonner and Bennett sat in their seats, ostensibly reading papers and paying no attention to the attack. Despite their brave front, the pressure was building. The opposition began to level more charges; the public as well as the RCMP was learning more. It was February 20, 1956, when Bonner finally admitted that an RCMP investigation had begun earlier in the month. Under relentless fire, he revealed that the RCMP report was expected soon, but it would not be filed in the House.

About this time, the opposition found another chink in Sommers' armour. He was responsible for mines as well as forests, and opposition members in committee claimed there had been nefarious goings-on in a northern mine road project. Sommers hedged and said he didn't have the report the opposition members cited. They replied they would return with the evidence.

When they did return, the mines minister was forced to admit to the House committee on mining that two contractors on a mining-road project in the north had hired his campaign manager from the 1953 election. In fact two people were hired: the ex-manager as timekeeper and his wife as cook. Sommers also said that the two contractors were personal friends who had been given the contract without it going to public tender. The Socred majority defeated by ten to six a motion to have Sommers ousted from the committee.

The continuing attack in the House was wearing Sommers down. Bennett was increasingly concerned about charges implicating himself in the affair and was well aware that Bonner's credibility was being chipped away.

An eloquent CCF member, Ron Harding, who had obtained by undisclosed means a copy of Sturdy's brief, said he was appalled at the seriousness of the charges. He stated, "If there was neither ineptitude nor bungling then we are witnesses to an extremely shrewd and clever piece of political manoeuvring and covering up by the attorney-general." Harding also contended that if there was anything to the charges, "it means absolute chaos in the forest industry in B.C. because there will have to be a review of every FML, every timber sale, every deal that passed over Sommers' desk."

Bennett fired back, once again sheltering behind the ongoing libel case against Sturdy, claiming the opposition had "all but destroyed the chances of an impartial hearing on the libel suit." But even his rock-solid demeanour was starting to crumble. He complained to the media about the opposition's "carping criticism" and the way they went "on and on like a babbling brook." The premier said he was very unhappy with the session and its lack of progress.

Before February ran out, however, Bennett made a move he hoped would stem the political hammering they were taking.

Sommers Toppled

As he had learned in the hardware business to move inventory when assets turned to liabilities, Bennett took a cool and ruthless look at the situation that now faced him. He had stood by Sommers for months because this was a man to whom he had given his trust and a key portfolio. Now accusations were piling up around Sommers, each one questioning his integrity, making his word seem worthless despite his new "Honest Bob" handle dreamed up by supporters. The situation threatened the government's touted image of purity as well as the reputation of Robert Bonner. Something must be done. It was time to isolate Sommers, to cut him off like a diseased limb threatening the solid Socred trunk.

On the night of February 27, Bennett called Sommers to a meeting in his office during the House dinner break. Bluntly he told him that until his name was cleared, he was out as minister. Bennett demanded an immediate resignation and said he would split the portfolio, giving lands and forests to Ray Williston and mines to Ken Kiernan. Sommers was shocked but didn't argue with the boss.

The entire legislature felt the tension when Robert Sommers rose at 10:10 p.m. to make a statement. For the next ten minutes Sommers virtuously tossed aside every criticism made against him, attacking with venom Gibson, Sturdy, and the publishers of the big city dailies whom he felt had pilloried him. It was vintage Sommers, sometimes scathingly bitter, sometimes in a trembling voice, he held the attention of the House. Bennett was grave and seldom took his eyes from Sommers, as the man he had trusted painted himself as a martyr, a victim, a blameless man, vilified and persecuted. His speech was extravagant, bordering on a diatribe, and in the end partially ineffective because he went too far. He led more than one listener to think "he doth protest too much."

Sommers told the legislature it was time to break his silence "on a matter which had been bruited about in this House in the most irresponsible and reprehensible manner, which was the subject of the most dirty and slanted coverage in the history of B.C., principally by Mr. Stuart Keate, the publisher of the *Victoria Times*." He added, "Ever since I took office as minister, my department and myself personally have been the subject of continuous and increasingly bitter attacks." Sommers claimed hundreds of thousands of dollars had been spent in a campaign of destruction against the government's forest policy and the FMLs. He accused Stu Keate of backing the "cut and get out" logging practices of small operators like Gordon Gibson. He stated that under Liberal leader Art Laing, some members of that party had "resorted to a campaign of distortion and falsehood that was without parallel in the political annals of this great province."

The opposition listened in stunned silence as Sommers contended the campaign against him was aimed at defeating the government. He said he was being continually discredited and his refusal to hit back was taken as a guilty confession. "Never at any time have I used my ministerial office for personal gain, either directly or indirectly, either morally or technically. To the best of my knowledge I have never, at any time, violated the oath of office that I felt I took on becoming a minister of the Crown," he stated.

Sommers claimed David Sturdy's appearance at the Sloan commission was a continuation of the assault by Gibson and was part of a Liberal conspiracy to oust the Socreds. He said he could not discuss the details of so-called evidence—blocked, of course, by his libel suit—but the members of the legislature might be interested in background. Eversfield had fled to California, Sommers charged, after being unsuccessful in trying to shake down his employer in Vancouver. He added that this once-trusted employee took with him photocopies of documents purporting to show "that the minister of lands and forests accepted bribes. Let me tell you that the charge is as phoney as the man who made it." He contended Eversfield had fled to the U.S. in order to escape prosecution.

The minister maintained his opponents sought a royal commission as "a vehicle for publishing hearsay and half-truths and a means of embarrassing and smearing individuals, groups and corporations." He said B.C. had recently experienced this type of damaging but ineffective inquiry, referring to the controversial Tupper Commission in Vancouver, which took place the year before to probe charges of corruption in the Vancouver police force. Eversfield may have followed the lead of Chief Walter Mulligan, who fled to Los Angeles as soon as he saw the writing on the wall.

Sommers said that if there had been a shred of evidence, Sturdy could have taken Eversfield to a local court clerk and sworn out an information charging Sommers with an offence. "Unfortunately, as Mr. Sturdy knows, there can be heavy penalties for false arrest and malicious prosecution," Sommers warned. He stated that attacks on himself and his ministry by Stu Keate, Art Laing, and his Liberals had occupied too much of the legislature's time. He concluded, "Because the public business of this province could have suffered through this irresponsible discussion and because this action will give me more opportunity to concentrate all my energies on this fight, I therefore now tender my resignation as Minister of Lands and Forests and Minister of Mines to the honourable premier."

Bennett's face was grim and expressionless, and some wondered if he would accept the resignation, unaware it had been ordered hours earlier. Bennett said only that he would have a statement later.

"You can really take it, Bob. You can take it," fellow Socred George Tomlinson told Sommers as several colleagues crowded around him in the corridor after he left the chamber. Some shook his hand, one slapped him on the shoulder, and others muttered quiet condolences. Sommers went to the legislative dining room with Gaglardi and did not return for the rest of the night session.

Such a spectacular resignation on the floor of the House had never been seen before. The opposition had expected denunciations and claims that Sommers was guiltless, but his resignation as minister was unexpected. MLAs wondered what it all meant. Some predicted an early election. Observers in the media commented on Bennett's brusque response to Sommers' resignation. They noted that the premier had not said he was sorry to receive it, nor had he paid any tribute to the minister's service to the government. Dillon O'Leary, a veteran reporter with the *Vancouver News Herald*, wrote, "It was considered, certainly by observers Monday night, that his resignation would be accepted by Bennett."

Urbane *Victoria Times* publisher Stu Keate was unrepentant, taking the resignation as a compliment to him and his paper. He said it was true that the *Times* had printed more about the case than most other newspapers. "I accept this as a tribute to the diligence of the *Times* staff in covering what was obviously a story of major importance to the people of B.C.," said Keate. He maintained that the paper actually had erred on the side of caution, and in fairness to Sommers had not printed other information it had uncovered. The Socreds had recently made allegations that Keate aspired to be the B.C. Liberal leader, and he now commented that three weeks earlier some prominent party members had approached him with this proposal because they felt Laing was a spent force. Keate said he rejected the overture because he "was a newspaperman, not a politician," and he remained one all his life.

Sommers the tree lord had been felled. Three days later the legislature was rocked by an attack from a reinvigorated opposition, but Wacky was soon in control again.

Furious Night

With Sommers twisting in the wind, the opposition was desperate to attack his statements, to keep the crisis boiling, to drive home to the public the message that bribery stalked the Socred stronghold. But the B.C. legislature operated on antiquated rules. There was no daily question period to give the opposition an opening for an assault. The premier set the agenda, and with his overwhelming majority he could change it as he chose. After Sommers' surprising statement, the premier quickly switched the agenda from a previously scheduled discussion of the forestry budget to a new topic. Anything to do with the Ministry of Lands and Forests would have provided an obvious opportunity for opposition questioning and attack. Some government members felt Bennett should have let the opposition make their assault immediately and then let the heat die down, but he played his own game. Bennett blithely explained, as he ignored mounting opposition anger, that there was other business he wanted cleared before the House adjourned later in the week.

Another ploy he used was legislation by exhaustion. On occasion he let the House sit long into the early morning hours, when tired opponents, out of words and out of energy, finally watched unwanted legislation rammed through.

The opposition waited through Tuesday and Wednesday as Bennett toyed with them. The caucus had discussed the merits of returning to the single-vote system rather than staying with the multiple-choice option that had been used in the past two elections. Several party members had pointed out that the system used to put them into office could also put them out if the votes were stacked against them. Changes were therefore proposed to the elections act that would mean a return to the one-person, one-vote formula. When the vote was called, the House approved a return to the old system almost unanimously.

Sommers was not in the House when the evening session began at 8:30 p.m. on March 1 with a discussion of ministry estimates. Ray Williston sat in his place as forests minister. It was perhaps ironic that Sommers had been replaced by another former schoolteacher and part-time musician. Williston at one time was the drummer of the Melody Five in the Interior town of Salmon Arm. He later kept the beat for his own band, Ray Williston and the Tickle Toes. He was quiet and friendly, a personal favourite of Bennett, respected for his integrity.

The proceedings began with long, rambling speeches on various issues by Bennett, Bonner, and Gaglardi. The restless opposition, knowing the premier planned to prorogue soon but also aware he couldn't avoid the forests ministry budget discussion, started yelling,

Ray Williston, a native of Victoria, was the MLA for Prince George. A former schoolteacher and principal, like Sommers, he started his political career as minister of education, then replaced Sommers as minister of lands and forests. He implemented Gordon Sloan's forest tenure recommendations and carried out Bennett's two-river policy involving the Columbia and Peace rivers.

"Filibuster, filibuster, filibuster." Bennett stuck to his game plan. He ran out the clock until 12:43 Friday morning, when he finally put the hot topic on the agenda and the donnybrook began.

The *Province* newspaper called it the "longest, loudest and most furious night in the history of the Legislature." It set a record as the longest sitting ever. There were long, angry harangues, vicious attacks, leather-lunged insults, smears, and charges. If there was an unused insult, it was purely an oversight. With the temperature at the boiling point, salvo after salvo was launched at the government, described variously as wicked, reckless, pernicious, and lying. Bruce Brown labelled Sommers a coward, withdrawing the word under protest when ordered to do so by Speaker Tom Irwin, who tried to keep the lid on tempers, frayed nerves, and what seemed like a mob scene. Through it all Bennett sat silent and steely eyed, growing greyer in the face as the long night wore on. The odd time he flashed his toothy smile and occasionally calmly sipped a cup of tea.

By early 1956 the Socred cabinet was changing, though some of the original 1952 ministers were still in place. From left to right: Les Peterson, Phil Gaglardi, Ray Williston, Ralph Chetwynd, Eric Martin, Ken Kiernan, W.A.C. Bennett, Robert Bonner, Wesley Black, Lyle Wicks, W.N. Chant, and E.C. Westwood.

Watching from the public gallery was Gordon Gibson, savouring the moment and wishing he could add his bellow to the bedlam. Gibson was one of the few who remained wide-awake the whole night as other spectators snoozed. The parliamentary restaurant ran out of bread and offered cheese and crackers. Larry Giovando, a medical doctor and independent member from Nanaimo, offered to dispense pep pills to any in need. He did a good business.

There were old charges and some new ones amid the yelling and shouting. The Speaker blocked Liberal MLA George Gregory's attempt to read out Sturdy's defence in the slander case. Bonner warned he could jeopardize his position as a lawyer and MLA if he did so. Gregory told the House that a "bucket shop" had bankrolled Sommers' trip east to see E.P. Taylor, naming Pacific Coast Services, Wick Gray's company. Bennett did not respond to repeated demands for a royal commission but hinted at what many had suspected would follow: an election. "This government is willing to go to the people at any time," the premier warned the House.

Even in his sleep, Phil Gaglardi was loud and made his presence felt. Slumped back in his seat for much of the night, his mouth open, his snoring sometimes could be heard rising above the angry voices and the noisy outbursts.

Through it all, the only cabinet member to come close to defending Sommers was his replacement, Ray Williston, who told hecklers that the entire issue was before the courts and no doubt "justice will be done." Williston charged that the opposition wasn't set up as a judge and jury and the issue would be dealt with at the proper venue. The CCF's Bob Strachan told Williston that the courts weren't something to hide behind.

Ernie Winch, elder CCF statesman and father of former party leader Harold, was one of the few who got a respectful hearing. He said an immediate inquiry wasn't called because the attorney general was afraid of what might be exposed. "This session has been the greatest disappointment in my political life. We are taught to look for honesty, democracy, and integrity in our governments. I have always respected this government and its members although I may have differed in opinion. But that respect has gone. They have failed to give to this principle that support which they will be mouthing on public platforms at the coming election," said Winch, a seasoned expert at predicting political moves.

By 6:20 a.m. Friday, the House had passed the previous record sitting of nine hours and 50 minutes established in April 1875. Members were snoozing at their desks, walking the corridors, and munching the diminishing supply of crackers. They wondered how long it would be before the Socred steamroller crushed the flagging opposition into submission. Socred John Tisdalle finally hauled himself to his feet and in a weary voice moved that the vote be put. It carried. There were still speeches to be made and insults to be hurled before B.C.'s longest sitting finally ended at 7:36 a.m. Most members were back in the House later in the day for the official end of the session. Cocky as ever, Bennett told reporters, "This is the best session we have ever had." It was all posturing. "When you can't fight policy, fight personality," Bennett gibed, dubbing the Liberals "a remnant of a great party."

In yet another angry editorial, the *Sun* said that the Socreds had turned their slogan "Social Credit Keeps You Informed" into a cynical joke, and the denial of an inquiry into the charges was a "flagrant affront to democracy." The *Province* also maintained that an inquiry was needed. "If nothing is done to deal with the charges in the Legislature, suspicion and rumour will compound and the public interest will not be served." It all rolled off the premier's back.

Bennett was confident that as long as he was creating jobs and good times, he could get the support of the voting public. Now political observers were left to wonder if his election hint was bluff or if, after only three years in office, he was prepared to go to the polls again. Would an election call be too obvious, designed to get in ahead of more scandals, more charges of bribery, and more revelations about the alleged skulduggery of Bob Sommers? The public waited.

The Police Report

The Sommers case became even murkier shortly after the House adjourned, when RCMP Inspector W.J. Butler delivered the first part of his report on the investigation into Sturdy's charges to the attorney general's department. Instead of taking it directly to Bonner, he merely left it at his office. The attorney general said later that he had not seen it. With its potential to harm the government, it is difficult to imagine Bonner not wanting to know immediately what the report contained, but he asserted he wanted department officials to make independent recommendations.

The Mountie's covering letter was revealing and drew attention to a specific paragraph in his report, which stated "there is definite indication of wrongdoing." It said Sommers, Gray, Schultz, and BCFP

Ken Kiernan moved from a garage and service station in Chilliwack to the ministry of agriculture and then mines. Along with Robert Bonner, Ray Williston, and Les Peterson, he became one of Bennett's longest-serving and most trusted ministers.

were involved. Butler had talked with Eversfield, examined his documents, and discussed details with forest administrators. The report referred to the possible use of fictitious names and invoices among Eversfield's papers.

The attorney general later stated that there was a tremendous difference between a "definite indication" and the "substantial evidence" that was needed before criminal charges could be laid. Nothing swayed Bonner from his position that the priority item was Sommers' libel suit against Sturdy. It remained before the courts and the attorney general steadfastly maintained it precluded any other action.

Even Sommers began to doubt the attorney general's strategy. In the early summer he and lawyer Alfred Bull went to Vancouver to meet with Bonner. Sommers was confident of his innocence and believed the case against him was so flimsy that it could be defeated in any court action. Bull agreed. They urged that Sommers be charged alone. Bonner would not agree. His position was that the role of his department was to prosecute crime, not to clear reputations. In political terms, a shaky case resulting in a quick acquittal would leave the public suspicious and questioning if justice had really been served. They might still wonder if it was simply a colossal cover-up. Some of the facts that might emerge from Sommers' civil action libel suit against Sturdy could clarify the situation, but the case was not scheduled to be heard until the fall.

So nothing changed, and Sommers was left in limbo with his fate still hanging in the balance. In addition, his financial situation had worsened. He had lost his ministerial pay and had only the sessional indemnity as income.

During the summer, the premier presided at the driving of the last spike in the extension of the PGE Railway into West and North Vancouver. Pulp and paper production was expected to expand by 327 percent over the next ten years, mining was on the upswing, and forest industry sales in 1955 were a record $631 million. The agricultural harvest was double what it had been ten years earlier. Secondary industry was growing rapidly, and Bennett even offered to annex the Yukon and part of the Northwest Territories in exchange for pushing the PGE to Whitehorse. Northerners told him to get lost.

Bennett's Peace River dreams gained substance as Westcoast Transmission announced it was planning a gas pipeline from the north to Vancouver. Some truly believed, as the government advertised, that the "fastest growing business in Canada" was the province of B.C.

Bennett made the most of some special dates—the 100th anniversary of the first sitting of the province's legislature, and the 26th anniversary of the opening of his Kelowna store, the cornerstone of his hardware empire. *Sun* reporter Frank Walden noted that for this occasion Bennett traded his habitual politician's dark suit for a light blue ensemble. Five hundred people paid 75 cents each to attend a tea-and-bun bash at the Kelowna Aquatic Club to honour Cec. He and his wife May cut a cake and rode in a "chartreuse-coloured convertible" at the head of a parade through town, accompanied by the skirling of the Legion pipe band. Sommers' black cloud didn't venture into the sunny Okanagan Valley skies.

During the anniversary festivities there was a riding nomination meeting. The delirious supporters gave a roaring unanimous vote to Bennett, the hometown boy. Again he talked election. "No one likes elections, but they are necessary," he told the faithful. "Every day an election is getting closer." Bennett knew he was going to like the next one because of soaring support. He touched on his favourite topic, debt retirement, promising that when he got rid of the awful inheritance left by the Coalition, "You will really see this Social Credit government go to town." In Kelowna his customers and friends didn't

Although the PGE had long been a joke in British Columbia–"Prince George, Eventually" was one of its nicknames when it seemed like the track would never continue north of Quesnel—Bennett was determined to complete the entire distance from North Vancouver to Prince George. In 1956, Bennett and Bonner were out to celebrate the completion of the southern extension into North Vancouver.

doubt him for a minute. He became furious when *Sun* editorial writers disbelieved his bookkeeping, and he challenged them to public debate. They didn't pick up his publicity-seeking gauntlet.

After a summer of pre-election palaver, on August 13 Bennett called an election for September 19. Other political leaders have paid the price for going to the polls early when there seemed no reason to do so, but Bennett was totally confident. He knew that the Liberals were in disarray, the Tories were dying, and the obvious opposition was the CCF, with Scottish immigrant Bob Strachan as its new leader. Strachan,

Bob Strachan, a carpenter from Nanaimo, was a more aggressive CCF leader than Arnold Webster and battled lustily with the Socreds in the 1956 election. However, his party was wracked by internal squabbles, which made it hard to keep the Socreds in focus as the enemy. When the smoke and fury cleared, the CCF had lost seats.

a carpenter, replaced the ineffective Arnold Webster, a gentle man who lacked the cut and thrust necessary in the Bennett era. Strachan was more boisterous, dubbed "the breeze from the Hebrides" by Bonner.

Bennett made vague statements about needing a strong mandate, which, of course, he already had. He was prepared to gamble, confident that the continuing boom of prosperity and another bulldozer-and-blacktop blitzkrieg would keep most of the people happy. Confusing, complex, vague, and unproven complaints about bribery and conspiracy would be no match for the juggernaut. Court officials stated publicly, three days after the election call, that there was a long waiting list and the Sommers libel case probably would not come up until November. Bennett's strategy was perfect. By then, the election would have come and gone.

The opposition knew Bennett held all the high cards; still they had no choice but to battle on. His timing left only the legal minimum of 38 days for campaigning. The electoral system had been completely overhauled. This time there would be a single vote rather than multiple choice. As well, new ridings had been added and candidates would contest 52 seats. The opposition screamed at the partition of the sparsely populated Peace River country into two ridings. These were two sure-fire seats for Bennett, who had been a booster for the region since he came to office and who was almost guaranteed most of the other back-country seats. At dissolution the House standing was 28 Socreds, 14 CCF, 4 Liberals, and 2 Independents. The two major parties charged into action, the Socreds with the slogan "Progress not Politics," and the CCF with "Let's Clean House."

Election 1956

Deane Finlayson's frustration was at the breaking point. The Conservative leader had feared that Bennett would push the election button before the public knew more about Sommers, and he was frustrated by the legal process in which the Court of Appeal had rejected Sturdy's bid to have the ex-minister give an immediate response to his libel charge. Despite all the accusations fired off in the last year and a half, there were signs that "Honest Bob" Sommers would have no trouble being re-elected in Rossland-Trail. Finlayson told a Vancouver audience on August 16 that despite the legal constraints, he planned to outline the nature of Sturdy's charges against Sommers at another public meeting in four days' time. Sommers' lawyer, Alfred Bull, warned that he would lay contempt charges if Finlayson followed through with his plans. Sturdy's lawyer, George Gregory, when confronted by the press about the threat of contempt charges against Finlayson, commented, "My reply is to ask you to tell Mr. Sommers to go jump in the lake." Finlayson said he was "not scared a bit."

The Tory leader took the plunge on Monday, August 20, before an expectant audience, disregarding Bull's contempt threat as promised. Speaking from a prepared text in St. John's Anglican Church hall in North Vancouver, with all the seats filled and many people turned away, Finlayson passionately lashed out at the Socreds. He knew he would get wide press coverage and headlines, although the *Province* newspaper declined to cover the meeting or print his claims because of the legal threats.

Finlayson said that in a six-month period Sommers had accepted $6,500 and a free trip to eastern Canada for himself and his family in exchange for issuing an FML. He flayed the premier for calling an election before the public knew the truth. "I do not recall this province ever having a premier who engaged in this wide-spread public deception year in and year out," Finlayson stated.

The Tory leader said he was not challenging Socred accomplishments but rather the way they were achieved, and he maintained the election was unnecessary. "The real reason for this election is to protect Mr. Bennett and his friends from discovery—discovery that what Mr. Bennett has been telling us about himself and the accomplishments of his government is not true," he told the applauding crowd.

Most of his statement was keyed to Bennett and the government and the question of honesty. Finlayson said he did not want his speech to be a smear or a libel, and he would read only the parts of Sturdy's charges "which are in fact the public business, the charges of misconduct which have been made against a minister of the Crown."

Finlayson cited payments of $2,500, $1,000, $2,000, and $1,000 to Sommers, along with the paid trip to eastern Canada. If the charges were not true, Bennett and Sommers should have acted quickly to clear them away, he contended. If they were true, it was Bennett's duty "to deal equally vigorously and speedily to right this wrong that was done."

A perspiring, elated Finlayson got thunderous applause and a standing ovation. Later in the week he sought the Conservative nomination in the riding of North Vancouver. On the strength of his gutsy action and performance, Finlayson had reason to think his chances for election were good, but some older, jaded political pros really wondered if his revelations would be enough. They had learned not to discount Bennett, regardless of the flak he faced.

What Finlayson said on the coast didn't matter at all in an equally packed, oven-hot hall in Trail that same night. Sommers basked in the adulation of a crowd of 200 who showed up for his riding nomination meeting. They roared, whistled, stamped their feet, and shook the Knights of Pythias Hall as Sommers told them, "When the facts are in there will be great sorrow in the enemy's camp." He knew of course that apart from Finlayson's threat, nothing more would be known of the affair until after the election. The court blockage continued to hold.

Sommers cried persecution but said he didn't mind "because I can fight back." Playing the role of martyr, sweat pouring down his face in the suffocating atmosphere, Sommers held the audience in the palm of his hand for more than an hour. He lashed out at political opponents and their propaganda campaign, their press pals, and vested interests in the forest industry, like Gibson, who opposed his policies. Sommers said the opposition had tried to laugh the Socreds out of contention and failed in 1952, and since then had used the "great, great smear." His nomination was unopposed. One lone voice cried "No," but the chairman said Sommers' election was unanimous.

In the smothering heat of the hall Sommers shouted, "Let the cold winds blow, I am thrilled beyond measure that you are not swayed by the political propaganda." He praised his supporters for standing fast. They carried him shoulder high through the hall as the crowd sang "For He's a Jolly Good Fellow" and Sommers wiped a tear from his eye.

Back in Vancouver, Alfred Bull immediately lay the threatened contempt action against Finlayson and the two newspapers that reported his speech. The *Sun* and the *News Herald* had provided the headlines; the *Province* had chickened out as it said it would. (The *News Herald* was a struggling morning paper that from its birth in the 1930s fought a non-stop battle against bankruptcy before dying in the late 1950s.) Little-known lawyer and MP John George Diefenbaker, soon to be Canada's prime minister, flew from Ottawa to defend Finlayson.

Mr. Justice J.O. Wilson heard the arguments. They were fairly brief, and with lightning speed, on August 28, he threw out Sommers' petition with scathing comments. The judge said Sommers' resignation speech was a "diatribe" and a "display of hyperbolic virtuosity." He added that Sommers had used a "whitewash brush for himself and a tar brush for his opponents." Judge Wilson said he was not pronouncing a general absolution for free discussion of the slander action, but was dealing only with the facts of this particular case. He referred to an attempt at strict press censorship by the Alberta Social Credit government in the 1930s that was thrown out by the Supreme Court of Canada. Wilson said it had been draconian legislation and quoted the Supreme Court's finding: "Democracy can not be maintained without its foundation, free public opinion and free discussion throughout the nation of all matters affecting the state within the limit set by the criminal code and the common law."

The opposition parties found some hope in the win against Sommers, although all the other signs looked bad. The *Sun*, in a wistfully optimistic editorial, wrote, "The Liberals strike at weak spots in Socred policies. Laing and his advisers have come up with a program that a whole lot of British Columbians will find difficult to reject." The *Sun* was wrong; the voters had no difficulty rejecting Laing's program.

The Socred bandwagon rolled along, propelled by wildly cheering crowds, particularly in rural areas. Bennett campaigned tirelessly, getting involved in a pushing match with the CCF candidate in Mission. The CCFer invaded the stage, claiming he had been maligned. In the yelling and shouting that followed, Bennett told a heckler, "I am your friend, my friend. I love this kind of meeting. Keep it up, all the love is on my side." The Socreds increasingly used television to hammer home their prosperity platform, and the premier crowed about their accomplishments.

Bennett steered clear of Sommers' riding and never appeared with him on any platform. The press noted it, but the faithful didn't care. In Kelowna, the premier had given qualified support to Sommers prior to the Trail nomination meeting. Bennett said that Sommers first had to get the support of the local people. "It is up to the local people to do the nominating, not me," Bennett stated, adding that Sommers was not charged with anything nor was he being sued by anyone. "He is trying to clear himself first with the local people, the highest court in the land under our democracy, and then in the court. He must do that before he comes back into cabinet," Bennett maintained. The premier told the crowd he was sure many people were praying for the former forests minister.

Bennett turned Shakespearean in defending himself against cover-up charges, quoting, "He who filches from me my good name robs me of that which not enriches him and makes me poor indeed." At another meeting he ran into 22-year-old Stephen Lewis, son of David Lewis and later the NDP leader in Ontario. Lewis heckled Bennett and shouted that he also could quote Shakespeare. "The evil that men do lives after them," he said. An infuriated Bennett shouted, "Finish, finish," but a laughing Lewis refused, leaving unsaid the poet's observation that "The good is oft interred with their bones."

When asked in Victoria if he was backing Sommers, Bennett referred to his previous statements. "You can read into them what you like," he declared. Bennett also classed as a Judas a Vancouver Socred who said Bennett had known early on about the forest licence bribery. "The greatest movement in the world's history had its Judas. We have had two or three," said Bennett, referring to one in particular, Ernest Allistone, a former president of the Socreds' Point Grey constituency. When he failed to get the nomination for his riding, Allistone was piqued and resigned from the party. His subsequent charges of wrongdoing in the forests ministry had Bennett steaming. Allistone didn't back down and claimed, according to a report in the *Sun*, that in September 1955, information about the forest scandal had been placed before the premier and Social Credit president Noel Murphy. Allistone also said that the Socreds' B.C. Free Enterprise Education Fund, headed by Einar Gunderson, was simply the party's slush fund, and he suggested that "these opportunists had their arms in the pork barrel not up to their elbows, but right up to their shoulders."

Some Socreds scrambled to distance themselves from the Sommers affair. Bible-banging Phil Gaglardi went right to the top, declaring he was a man of God and therefore would have nothing to do with anything unclean. Liberal leader Art Laing came up with another of his classically inaccurate predictions, maintaining that Socred handling of the Sommers affair meant, "win, lose or draw on September 19, they're through." Bennett modestly predicted he might get three more seats. A final Vancouver rally packed 2,500 into the Georgia Auditorium for a night of acclaim, exaggeration, promises, wild applause, and confidence. Outside a rube band entertained those who couldn't get in, and communists handed out pamphlets to the few who would take them. The meeting went on so long that ushers who were hired to take up a silver collection quit and went home without passing the plate.

Although they knew their campaigns were dying, opposition candidates battled on, and Bonner was often their target. The CCF's Bob Strachan, electioneering in the Interior, delivered a delightfully alliterative assault on the attorney general and Bennett. The "Hebridean Breeze" howled that Sommers' role was still unclear, "but we have been concerned with the bumptious, bungling Bonner, and the peremptory, presumptuous premier."

It was a landslide, a win that not only solidified Bennett's party but also crushed all opposition. Laing and Finlayson were among those swept away. Instead of 3 seats, Bennett gained 11 and wound up with 39 of the House's 52 seats. The CCF won only 10, a loss of 4; Liberal strength was reduced from 4 to 2, and Finlayson's support disappeared. Tom Uphill was again the lone Independent. The Socreds, however, got only 44.9 percent of the popular vote, despite the collapse of the once-powerful Tories who polled a minuscule 3.9 percent. The CCF got 24.2 and the Liberals 20.9. Wacky had again waltzed in on a split vote.

Sommers won effortlessly. He led from the first poll to the last, and within the first hour of vote counting, victory was his. He nervously smoked non-stop as returns came in. His supporters roared and cheered with a long outburst when it was reported Finlayson was trailing badly in North Vancouver. "Hooray," shouted Sommers.

In a ringing cry of outrageous extravagance, Bennett declared, "It is the greatest victory for the ordinary people since the Magna Carta." Wacky laughed that he had beaten not only the other parties but also the Canadian Broadcasting Corporation, whose reporting he had come

Tom Uphill was the Independent member for East Kootenay from the 1920s until 1960, becoming the longest-sitting member in the history of the B.C. legislature. Although a Labour candidate, the man from Fernie supported Bennett and the Socreds over Harold Winch's CCF in the 1952 minority government situation. He charted his own path, siding now with the socialists, now with the free-enterprisers.

to dislike, and the metropolitan press. "The *Vancouver Sun* has really set," he chortled.

Laing noted philosophically, "The people admire the boldness and even the recklessness of the government. Talking caution probably cost us votes." It was an odd claim because the Liberals had battled the "libel stonewall" as hard as they could.

Finlayson found his political career totally crushed, his dream gone, his worst fears realized. He was devastated and blunt. "Fascism is taking root. What in God's name is the matter with the people of this province?" Finlayson pointed to three characteristics of the electorate that spelled his downfall: political immaturity, materialism, and non-appreciation of political principles.

The CCF's Bob Strachan, like Laing, was philosophically pragmatic. "Money beat us; people are not interested in democracy any more, they just want a half-mile of blacktop."

The *Sun* said that at least the province could look forward to five years of political stability.

Bennett, cock-of-the-walk, had humiliated the opposition and now his opportunities seemed unlimited. He braced himself for new battles with Ottawa over water and hydro projects. Only one thing haunted him: he wasn't rid of the Sommers problem. When he revamped his cabinet, Bob wasn't in it, but his presence as an MLA in Victoria was the spectre that continued to hang over Bennett and his government.

Pipe Dreams and Power

British Columbians were starting to regard the Sommers affair as a modern Hundred Years' War. The skirmishing went on and on. Just one month after the third Socred election victory, in October 1956, Mr. Justice Harry Williams gave David Sturdy permission to look into Sommers' bank accounts in Victoria and Vancouver. Sommers appealed the decision to the Supreme Court of Canada, causing another delay in the proceedings, but Judge Williams' decision was eventually upheld.

During the fall of 1956 and spring 1957, Sommers was a quiet backbencher but a constant reminder of unresolved issues. His situation did not dominate the session, but Liberal George Gregory continued his attacks. On March 6, 1957, referring to Inspector W.J. Butler's still-secret RCMP report, Gregory said one of Eversfield's documents showed that Sommers accepted $6,500 in loans over a five-month period, from a firm that "existed for no other purpose than to assist its clients in getting forest management licences." Gregory then demanded that Bonner table the RCMP report and prosecute Sommers.

Bonner insisted that the Butler report would not be made public because that would be contrary to common practice and he was not prepared to divulge its contents. He did make one small concession, admitting that Sommers' claim in his resignation speech of a conspiracy to wreck the government contained "considerable poetic licence."

Throughout the Sommers affair, all the Socreds and some CCF members felt that Gordon Gibson's early charges in the legislature were merely politics and the ranting of a loud mouth. His accusations were explained away as a Liberal conspiracy, probably engineered in the East, to discredit the Socred government and bring about its downfall in the next election. In the beginning, Socred members believed the charges were complete fabrication, but Eversfield's documents gave weight to the Liberal cause, and Gordon Gibson, along with other influential and wealthy members of the party, came up with the funds needed to find new fuel for their arguments. In the political paranoia that existed at the time, the Socred caucus felt it was being unfairly attacked from every direction, so it also felt justified in putting into practice any strategy that kept the hounds at bay—including any delaying tactics Bonner could think up. They believed

The Socreds and their opposition looked calm and civilized in the elegant surroundings of the B.C. legislature as yet another session opened in 1957, but the cut-and-thrust was not far beneath the surface.

they were simply fighting off another injustice perpetrated by the old established parties.

With a five-year mandate, Bennett ignored the jibes that came from the floor of the legislature and from other political arenas. In November, Deane Finlayson told the annual meeting of the provincial Tories, now without a seat in the House, "The only purpose that can be achieved by the voters supporting Social Credit is to divide Canada and split Western Canada off from the East." Visiting Ontario Tory MP Donald Fleming, who later became a federal minister, told reporters the party was a "nuisance."

Before the end of the year there was exciting news to bolster Bennett's northern dreams. A major gas find was announced in the Peace River district, meaning there would be millions of dollars pouring into the northeast, creating hundreds of new jobs. Financial figures for the year were excellent: forest income was forecast at $640 million; mining, fishing, and secondary industries were all expanding; and there was a dramatic increase in construction. A confident public went on a spending spree.

When the legislature met early in 1957, a reduced, dispirited opposition faced the cocky Socreds. Bennett gave a low-key Throne

Speech, offering encouragement for steel-industry expansion and promising more courts for an overloaded justice system. As an outsider who was no longer a member of one of the leading national parties, Premier Bennett took every opportunity to lash out at the federal government, especially when he found that the public agreed with him. Just as many B.C. premiers have done before and since, he accused Ottawa of taking more in taxes from the province than was ever returned for government programs.

The cautious budget, as Bennett called it, reflected a temporary downturn in the forest industry resulting from a 10 percent decrease in both production and sales. In order to improve the government's financial position, he promised to extend the coverage of the 10 percent forest and mining tax he had imposed in 1953. Then he spent the increased revenue, and the opposition screamed that he was trying to fool the people by giving them back their own money. Bennett introduced a $28-a-year tax reduction for 267,000 homeowners. It was welcomed by the voters, and succeeding governments have increased it ever since. The premier also planned a 50-mile northern extension of his beloved PGE Railway and a provincial debt-reduction scheme.

Bennett's dreams of massive hydro-electric development to power industrial expansion in B.C. were garnering interest around the world. He expressed a desire to develop power from both the Columbia and Peace rivers at the same time, a two-river policy that critics said was financially impossible. The Canadian and U.S. governments wanted to develop the Columbia, which twisted its way through both countries, with no regard for the distant Peace, which rises in northeastern B.C. and flows through Alberta on its way to the Arctic. Bennett bristled at what he felt was interference from Ottawa and a disregard for the province's wishes for the Columbia, which he saw as a provincial resource. He also believed he could finance the Peace River project more easily if a favourable deal with the U.S. could be struck first on the Columbia.

The Columbia dispute filled the papers for years, as Bennett battled Ottawa and thwarted the desires of Canada and the U.S. by demanding conditions that favoured B.C. In the end, he won. The complicated Columbia River treaty was not finally ratified until the premier got the deal he wanted. They said it couldn't be done, but Bennett got his two-river policy.

Capitalizing on every opportunity, Bennett proceeded to amaze the opposition with his own impersonation of the Wizard of Oz, leading

B.C. down the Yellow Brick Road to a wonderland in his favoured northeastern region of the province. On February 21, 1957, Sommers' successor, Lands and Forests Minister Ray Williston, drew worldwide reaction when he announced that the government was considering a massive project in the northeast, tabling in the legislature a memorandum for a gigantic development scheme. Of breathtaking proportions, it was to be undertaken by a government-industry consortium headed by a mysterious man from Sweden named Axel Wenner-Gren, a male equivalent of the Wicked Witch, according to critics. Wenner-Gren, with international interests in pulp and paper, mining, food processing, real estate, and appliance manufacturing, had sent emissaries to B.C. to investigate resource development after hearing of the area's rich natural potential. Bennett liked the man's imagination and daring, and within months the Wenner-Gren Development Corporation was created and registered.

The scenario presented to the legislature by Williston was almost unbelievable. Slated for development were 40,000 square miles within the Rocky Mountain Trench, 10 percent of B.C.'s land mass. The Wenner-Gren Corporation would build a railway to the Yukon, and in exchange would receive forest and mineral rights in the area. A pulp mill and hydro-electric development were under consideration. When Williston envisioned a billion-dollar, ultra-modern monorail racing at 160-miles-an-hour through the north to the Yukon border, skeptics had a field day. They said it was a fast train to nowhere. A $5 million survey of the area was to be undertaken within two years.

Opponents said Bennett planned to crown the man from Sweden as Emperor Axel, Supreme Ruler of the Rocky Mountain Trench. Labour unions worried about the possibility of immigrant workers being brought in for the project, newspaper reporters tried to find out how much money was involved, and one Victoria paper said a poll of readers showed there were 1,400 doubters compared to 80 people who supported the project or thought it was realistic.

As soon as the memorandum of intent was filed with a $500,000 deposit, critics roared "giveaway." Their extravagant condemnations matched the superlatives of Bennett and his government. Most northerners, even good Socred supporters, adopted a "show-me" attitude, although some shared Bennett's dreams, and minor entrepreneurs headed north to sniff out opportunities. Whether the Wenner-Gren project was real or a fantasy, it grabbed the headlines and kept the media spotlight off Bob Sommers. Lost in the rhetoric was the fact that, initially, it was only a memorandum of intent.

The presence on the new corporation's board of directors of Einar Gunderson, defeated politician but still Bennett's close confidant, spurred both Vancouver and Victoria newspapers to produce editorials about conflict of interest. Gunderson's established role was financial fixer and party bagman. He was also vice-president of the provincially owned PGE and director of the Toll Highways and Bridges Authority. Political opponents charged him with a conflict of interest, although they might more accurately have mentioned the phrase "political patronage," which Bennett only five short years previously had been so set against. The premier came to the defence of his friend, calling him "that great Canadian—there is no finer man in B.C." He claimed Gunderson was the target of smears and McCarthyism.

Within a few days the press began to take a closer look at Wenner-Gren and found a clouded history and considerable criticism of him in Europe. He had maintained close business ties with Nazi Germany and had profited from selling arms and supplies during the Second World War. It was little more than ten years since the carnage ended, and many vivid memories remained. Most people in B.C. were antagonistic towards Nazi collaboration or the suggestion of it. Newspaper reports about the man's ties to the Hitler regime probably raised more anger than the suggestions of a massive resource giveaway by Bennett. Several years later there were arguments that Wenner-Gren had been maligned, but by then he was gone.

The consortium collapsed quickly, mired in financial uncertainty. There were those who contended that Bennett never thought for a minute that the Wenner-Gren scheme would come to fruition because of its enormous scale and the amounts of money required. If there were some investment and jobs created, so much the better. The major benefit was that the proposed scheme brought the potential of the area to the attention of international financiers who had never before known it existed.

Bennett's own plans for hydro-electric development of the Peace River region appeared modest and achievable after the extravagance of the Wenner-Gren plan, so he was more easily able to proceed with them. His government subsequently built the mammoth Bennett Dam, resulting in the creation of Williston Lake, at more than 200 miles long, the largest in B.C. and a massive source of hydro-electric power.

In June 1957 the *Vancouver News Herald* died, and the *Vancouver Sun* moved in with the Southam-owned *Vancouver Province*, sharing the new Pacific Press building at 2250 Granville Street through a joint operating agreement. Though the *Sun* was still locally owned, Bennett could now damn his "Number One Enemy" as an ally of eastern Canadian interests.

As always in B.C. there was a personal issue that caught the public's attention, pushing Sommers aside. The great beer parlour crisis of '57 was fanned into flame by the threat to end the 10-cent glass of suds. The 392-member B.C. Hotel Association wanted to hike the price of a glass to 15 cents and to introduce a 25-cent glass that would hold two-and-a-half times the amount of the 10-center. They asked the government for permission to raise the price of beer. The Association claimed members were being killed by higher prices for beer and labour. Beer-parlour patrons foamed in fury. "No way," they cried.

Bennett, who knew the importance of the beer-drinking voter, also said "no." The hotelmen came back with a barrel-load of complicated price proposals—enough to drive a person to drink. They argued that bigger glasses would mean less tap-drip loss and less costly breakage. Nobody really believed them, and finally the government negotiated a compromise and ruled the beloved 10-center would stay, along with a bigger glass, a 20-center.

Enterprising *Sun* reporter Ed Moyer, no mean sipper, had the suds hitting the fan with a simple experiment. He proved, complete with pictures, that the beer in a 20-center wouldn't fill two 10-centers. Ed said the wider neck on the bigger glass produced a lot of foam and less beer. Beleaguered by beer and its problems, Hotel Association president J.J. Castock said that if the collar on a big glass—the space between the suds and the brim—was more than half an inch, the buyer should send it back. Fistfights broke out in some parlours between drinkers and innkeepers. The two-glass system remained. Of such things are B.C. crises made.

Bennett slapped a 10 percent tax on 24 bingo club operators in Vancouver, where patrons were reported spending, on average, a whopping six dollars per night. The violent, bomb-planting, house-burning, Sons of Freedom Doukhobor sect tied up police in Sommers' part of the world, the Kootenays, as hundreds of them, charging

On September 12, 1965, W.A.C. Bennett sat in the dumptruck that deposited the last load of fill on the dam (below) named in his honour. To realize his dream of a power project in northeastern B.C., the premier took a leaf from the CCF book and nationalized B.C. Electric and Peace Power, creating the B.C. Hydro and Power Authority.

persecution, proclaimed they wanted to leave B.C. and go back to Russia from whence they came earlier in the century. It was all bluff; they never left the Kootenays. These events kept the public's attention off Sommers as the summer passed, and everyone enjoyed the sunshine at the beach.

The Sloan Report

Bennett was furious and Judge Sloan unhappy when tenacious *Sun* reporter, Alex Young, beat his colleagues with a September 5, 1957, scoop on the eagerly awaited inquiry report. Industry executives and labour leaders tried to interpret the judge's findings as reported by Young while the massive 888-page document awaited official release. For Judge Sloan it was a replay from nine years earlier when *Sun* columnist James K. Nesbitt jumped the gun in 1948 with a scoop on his first report. Young's story came only two days after the judge delivered his report to the government. It was never discovered who leaked it, despite an intensive investigation, nor was it learned if the leak came from the same source as the one nine years earlier.

After two-and-a-half years of hearings, which ran simultaneously with heated debates in the legislature about the Sommers affair, Judge Sloan decided that his original recommendations weren't perfect, but, he said, "the system works." The need for refinements and repairs was obvious, however, the main problem being the government's lack of any clear procedure for granting licences. Sloan said regulations should be drafted that would ensure licences were granted on an "equal basis," and he also called for a well-defined list of priorities for all applications, adding that all interested parties from communities involved should be given a chance to be heard.

Sloan said that 23 licences had so far been issued, and he recommended that the 21 applications currently before the government be approved as soon as they were certified by ministry staff. He said that no more licences should be considered for five years and that in future they should be granted for a period of 21 years and not in perpetuity as earlier ones had been. He made one exception to the moratorium and recommended that small operators should not have to wait the five years; instead, they could apply immediately for licences on public sustained yield units (PSYUs, the new name for working circles). PSYU licences would be granted to those who "sell logs in the open market and who meet the requirements of [running] mills with no timber of their own." He also advocated a permanent forestry advisory committee be set up; a recommendation he had made in his first report.

Sloan said that tax relief for the forest industry was a must, "as it bears all the taxation it can stand." While he doubted blackmail or bribery was rampant, he urged the government to ensure that it didn't exist in timber auctions because it was an "evil" that must be stamped out. He recommended the survey of timber potential in each forest area be improved so there would be a more accurate assessment of the amount of wood available. He announced that future licences would be called Tree Farm Licences (TFLs). At least 15 percent and as much as 30 percent of the annual allowable cut for each TFL was to be allocated to small loggers. One of the provisions he wanted to add to new TFLs was that they set aside "reserves of timber within the licence area for the supply of other industries," but this practice was never implemented.

When the media approached H.R. MacMillan for his reaction, he said he was unhappy with the report because this system would increase the number of TFLs, which would further encroach on the amount of Crown land set aside for small loggers. MacMillan contended that although the report urged a 30 percent allocation for small loggers in all TFLs, there would be fewer circles in total and it would be a net loss for the little guy. All of the productive available forest in the Vancouver Forest District was gradually being allocated for TFLs that were offered to large corporations with access to large amounts of capital. MacMillan favoured an overall expansion of working circles or PSYUs on Crown lands, and he felt Sloan's recommendations would in time amount to a reduction. He predicted the loggers would become mere sharecroppers in the system, working for the big guys.

When an irate government finally released the report, it was a five-dollar bestseller. The *Sun* hailed it as a Bill of Rights for small loggers, who temporarily were satisfied with Sloan's recommendations. There were, however, some tight smiles in industry circles, as Sloan's report shortened tenure, increased costs, and restricted company control. In fact, these TFLs issued with a provision for review every 21 years provided no secure tenure for the large forest companies and would in the next 40 years do much to frustrate both government and the industry. Sloan, like MacMillan, felt the forest service was understaffed, overworked, and underpaid and recommended higher wages for foresters than for other civil servants as a means of improving the situation.

At this time over one-third of provincial revenue came from the forest industry. Sloan reported that the sector paid about $38 million a year in provincial sales tax, plus $28 million in stumpage and royalties. The B.C. government at that time ploughed back about one-third of this amount to pay for administration, protection, and rebuilding the forests. He also pointed out that the federal government collected $112 million a year from the forest industry, returning less than one percent to the province.

On September 9, as news of the new TFLs faded from the front pages of newspapers, Premier Bennett called three by-elections to fill vacancies that had occurred in recent months. The Liberal executive sent the unfortunate Arthur Laing on a kamikaze mission, insisting that he run for the Burnaby vacancy created by the death of Ernie Winch. Defeat would give them the final reason for dumping him as leader. Laing ran a humiliating fourth behind the CCF, Socred, and Tory contenders. It was all over, although he didn't relinquish the title of leader until 1959, primarily because nobody else wanted the job. A sincere, hard-working, but uncharismatic man, his redemption came when he returned to the federal fold as an MP with a seat in Prime Minister Lester Pearson's cabinet and a later appointment as a minister in Prime Minister Pierre Trudeau's government. His most important posting was as minister of Indian Affairs and Northern Development.

Where's Waldo?

While there were many bizarre twists and turns in the protracted Sommers saga, the fall of 1957 produced one of the more curious ones. As the by-election campaigns got underway, Sommers disappeared. He had gone quietly about his business as a backbench MLA, and some of his confidence seemed restored, but he was suffering from the stress of being constantly under the gun. In September he failed to appear for the annual meeting of the Rossland-Trail riding association. He sent a wire from Victoria stating he was ill.

In the continuing court battle, Sturdy had finally applied to the Supreme Court of B.C. to have Sommers appear quickly or have his libel case thrown out. Sommers was ordered to attend a pre-trial hearing on September 23. His new lawyer, Jim Proudfoot of Victoria, told reporters, "Mr. Sommers is a very sick man and the strain of examination might give him a heart attack." In an interview at their Victoria home, Sommers' wife, Nona, stated, "I am the only one who knows where he is and I'm not going to tell anyone. I don't care what happens to the case. I'm going to protect my husband. He is a very sick man. I am sure any wife in my position would do the same." That summer Sommers and his family had moved to a new, modestly priced, $12,900 Victoria home. Mrs. Sommers told questioning reporters that he had put it in her name, presumably to prevent a claim on the family assets if he lost his legal battles.

Yet another Sommers' lawyer, Lorne Jackson, provided the court with a medical certificate dated August 22, signed by Dr. V. Goresky of Castlegar. It said Sommers was suffering from paroxysmal tachycardia—sudden attacks of rapid heartbeating—and migraine headaches brought on by excessive nervous strain. The doctor wrote that, in his opinion, Sommers needed at least four months' rest and the avoidance of all controversial matters. The presiding judge dismissed the doctor's note, a common practice in this era when only recognized illnesses were accepted by judges as valid excuses for postponing a trial. A communicable disease, an urgent operation, or a high fever were acceptable excuses; heart palpitations and other less definable illnesses were not. The judge noted that if the medical opinion was accepted, Sommers could be free of any future court action. He ordered another pre-trial hearing for October 7, with the trial scheduled to start two weeks later.

Sommers, however, had vanished. On October 21 he was given another week to prove he was sick or to show up. "This is just a straight disregard of the order of the court," said the judge, J.V. Clyne. Sommers didn't show up on the 28th and the case was thrown out.

David Sturdy's lawyers tried to bring out additional information in court but were prevented from doing so by Clyne, who said they had already won their case. "Sturdy said the plaintiff took bribes and his words were true and the plaintiff's action has now been dismissed," Clyne added.

Sturdy was vindicated but unhappy. "I feel I have won the case but it is not as good as winning it in court," said the lawyer, who had hoped for a court battle to bring out all the evidence against Sommers.

But with the end of the libel suit, the floodgates were finally opened, all barriers removed, and the case against Sommers began to unfold in its entirety. The documents filed by Sturdy were released by the court and became available to the press and so to the public. Particularly damaging was a letter to Sturdy written by Charles Eversfield from his home in Los Angeles, dated November 1955. He wrote that shortly after Sommers got the forestry job, Wick Gray brought him to the PCS office in Vancouver. "It was either shortly before or shortly after this time that there was noticeable interest in Mr. Gray's office in the granting of FMLs," Eversfield wrote. (When a company sought an FML, it generally hired a consulting firm such as Schultz and Associates to prepare the documentation required for the application. Eversfield seems to suggest here that companies applying for an FML were now hiring Gray's company to ensure their applications went through.) Eversfield wrote that three or four months later, after Gray made several visits to Victoria, he heard his boss state, "I am in charge of the 'dinging' department."

Eversfield also wrote that by April 1953 it was taken for granted that money for Sommers would be funnelled through Wick Gray's companies. The first payment was $15,500 from BCFP in November 1953. The accountant said the money was to be divided equally between Gray's PCS and Sommers. It would be declared as income and Sommers would kick in part of the tax to be paid. Sommers actually got $5,125 at this time. The half received by PCS was deposited to Evergreen Lumber Sales, a Gray company, for eventual payment to Sommers through complicated financial transactions involving Wick's brother, John Gray. Eversfield maintained this was just one example of financial juggling, and he had photocopies of the relevant documents. His letter did not indicate whether the BCFP money was a direct payment or if it came through C.D. Schultz and Associates.

Eversfield's papers indicated that the amount of money involved might be much larger than previously anticipated, with Sommers slated to receive about $40,000, the money allegedly coming from such PCS clients as BCFP, Tahsis, Empire Mills, Church Sawmill, and the East Asiatic Company. One of the documents released to the media alleged the split of $193,087 between H. Wilson Gray, Robert E. Sommers, and C.D. Schultz.

The newspaper stories dealing with the documents were long and convoluted, suggesting that fairly large amounts of money had been paid, but for what, by whom, and even when the payments were made was far from clear to readers, who would have to wait for an inquiry or a trial to learn more.

While his name was prominent in every provincial daily newspaper, Sommers was still in hiding. He was in the United States, living for most of the time with his daughter in California. Nevertheless, he needed funds and at one point contacted Waldo Skillings, asking

Net Earnings	#1 HWG	#3 R.E. Sommers	#2 C.D. Schultz
To date	25,196		17,696
	6,299	18,897	
	31,495	18,897	17,696
Confirmed	15,000		15,000
	3,750	11,250	
	50,245	30,147	32,696
Projected	26,666		26,667
	6,667	20,000	
	83,578	50,147	59,363
	83,578		
	50,147		
	59,363		
Total	193,088		

This worksheet prepared by Charles Eversfield was one of more than 1,000 documents entered in evidence when Sommers finally came to trial. The figures in the document were never substantiated and are far in excess of the approximately $7,000 Robert Sommers was convicted of receiving. Eversfield's documents constituted much of the evidence on which the original 50 charges (later greatly reduced) against the four accused were based.

him to perform a peculiar and hard-to-believe favour that was kept secret until long after the events.

Skillings was a Socred supporter from Victoria with ambitions to become an MLA. He had known Sommers for more than 25 years, beginning when they were both student teachers. Sommers had not spoken to Bennett or Bonner before skipping to the U.S., but he phoned Skillings in October, saying he was in Seattle, broke and needing money.

Skillings' role in the Sommers affair is intriguing, mysterious, and full of contradictions. Sommers' recollections do not jibe with what Skillings, a close friend of Premier Bennett, later a Socred MLA and cabinet minister, disclosed years later. Skillings stated that Sommers' asked him to get in touch with Gordon Wismer, former attorney general in the Coalition government, who would put him in touch with a group

Waldo Skillings knew and admired Bennett from the days of the Coalition government, when Bennett was a Tory member and Skillings a Tory supporter. When Bennett moved to the Socreds, his friend helped run the election campaign. Skillings was finally elected as a Socred in 1960, becoming party whip and, later, minister of industrial development, trade, and commerce. He sat—or slept—through debates beside another colourful colleague, Phil Gaglardi.

of influential people who didn't want to see Sommers starve. A former political opponent, Wismer would seem to be an unlikely friend or ally for a Socred in trouble.

The account becomes more bizarre. Skillings contended that he went to Seattle with $25,000 cash in a money belt. Sommers refused to accept it because he would have to sign for it. The cash apparently was returned to the donors in Vancouver.

Sommers' version is that Skillings approached him with an offer of a lifetime pension of $600 per month, allegedly put up by a group of Socred supporters who wanted him to stay out of the country in the hope that the controversy at home would die down and remove the pressure from the premier and his government.

When Skillings told Bennett his version of events, the premier was reported to be furious and baffled as to why Skillings would get involved in such a deal with all its potential for further political disaster.

Regardless of which version is correct, if this story had been known at the time, the fact that money had been offered to Sommers would have produced fresh fodder for the rumour mills and his political opponents. It seems unlikely that either $25,000 cash or a $600-a-month lifetime pension would have been enough to keep Sommers in the U.S. indefinitely. The tale is confusing and difficult to follow, but like so much in this part of the story, there are hints and suggestions that others were involved who remained undetected in the shadows. As Skillings ruefully commented years later, "In the political racket you can't believe anything you hear."

Sommers' Return

While Skillings was acting as a courier for Sommers, the premier was under increasing pressure from politicians and the media to act. The dismissal of the libel case prompted loud, immediate demands for the government to lay charges. Bonner was in Europe with a trade mission and could not be reached, but the acting attorney general, Les Peterson, took some of the heat off by telling the media that "the possibility of a legal inquiry has not been ruled out."

Reporters went to other sources for answers. Mrs. Sommers still wouldn't say where her husband was, and she stuck by him without question. She was sure he would clear himself and she expected him home by Christmas. In his riding, Angus Drinnan, president of the Rossland-Trail Socred Association, said that until he heard from his constituents he would "sit tight." Rather plaintively, Drinnan noted that not knowing where Sommers was "makes things a little awkward at times."

Bennett looked unusually tired and grim as he held a series of hurried meetings with individual ministers and then his full cabinet on October 31. The cabinet decided to ask Mr. Justice Gordon Sloan, who had less than two months previously handed in his review of forest legislation, to open another royal commission hearing on the Sommers allegations. Sloan was immediately contacted by telephone and arrived at the parliament buildings just before the cabinet meeting broke. Bennett handed him the ticking time bomb and the judge reluctantly accepted.

Sloan questioned whether the provincial government had legal authority to set up the inquiry, and he said at the outset that he wanted to check it with the relatively new federal justice minister, Davie Fulton, who happened to be from Kamloops. Sloan wanted to be sure he would not compromise himself by assuming a key role in this sensitive political case, which he felt could fall under federal jurisdiction. Fulton told him the inquiry was in order.

Bennett hated press conferences but was forced to call one. He was totally subdued, sitting much of the time with his chin on his chest. There still was the odd flash of the old Bennett bravado during the twenty-minute session, but much of the time was taken up by the reading of the indictment. It was signed first by acting-Attorney General Les Peterson in Bonner's absence, then by Bennett and eight other cabinet ministers. It stated that the commissioner was to inquire if money was paid to Sommers to influence his granting of FMLs. Six companies were named for investigation: B.C. Forest Products Ltd., Tahsis Company, Empire Mills Ltd., C.D. Schultz and Associates, Pacific Coast Services, and Evergreen Ltd. (the last two both Wick Gray companies). The media noted that two other companies cited in Charles Eversfield's affidavit were not mentioned, Church Sawmills and the East Asiatic Company. Eversfield had maintained Church paid $5,000 and East Asiatic $45,000.

Bennett parried reporters' questions, but he failed to repeat his usual comment about Bonner being Canada's youngest and smartest attorney general. Asked about Bonner, Bennett pointedly stated, "My friend, the attorney general is the attorney general and the government has acted on his recommendation." The media wondered if Bennett's steadfast support of Bonner was waning.

Sloan appointed county court prosecutor Stanley J. Remnant as prosecutor for the commission, which was scheduled to open in Victoria on November 12. There were some optimistic calculations that the inquiry would last about a month. It didn't. This time it was shorter. Despite all the excitement about the Sommers affair, there were only ten spectators along with a horde of newsmen as the session opened with a scrap between two lawyers. One of them, Alfred Bull, had represented Sommers in the libel suit, but now Charlie Schultz was his client. Bull objected to Sturdy's bid to represent Eversfield because he was personally involved in the case.

While this issue was placed under advisement, Bull brought the pot to a boil, saying he would seek an injunction to block the inquiry because it was unconstitutional. This was the niggling thought that had made Judge Sloan reluctant to become commissioner. Bull argued that only the federal government could make a decision in criminal matters, and yet the commission, a criminal inquiry, had been ordered under provincial law. Judge Sloan immediately ordered a four-week adjournment until December 8. In Ottawa, Justice Minister Davie Fulton repeated that the Sloan inquiry was properly constituted and it caused him no problem. Despite this, Bull told reporters he was planning to launch his request for an injunction within a few days.

While this latest legal challenge got underway in Victoria, Sommers, responding to entreaties from his family, suddenly returned to B.C. on November 12. He had been missing since August 28. A story in the *Sun* describing his homecoming suggested that at least one reporter had been tipped off.

According to the report, which appeared without a by-line, Sommers hit the border at the Douglas crossing in a two-tone, fawn-coloured, 1954 Monarch with licence plate number 2050. No details were omitted. With the reporter in hot pursuit, Sommers drove through Vancouver and over the Lions Gate Bridge to Horseshoe Bay, where he bought a ticket for the ferry to Nanaimo. Before boarding, he made a phone call. "Before he entered the booth he made a careful scrutiny of the area, glancing at people sitting in their parked cars," readers were told. It could have been he was simply looking for a phone booth, but that was obviously not dramatic enough for the tale.

Sommers then boarded the ferry and took a twisting route through Nanaimo after he landed, several times pulling into side streets and turning off his lights. Supposedly he was looking to see if he was being followed, the report suggested. Finally he made the dash down the Island to Victoria.

Next morning there was a lively scene outside the bungalow at 3 Obed Avenue as a half-dozen cars full of reporters and photographers laid siege to the Sommers home. Breathless radio reporters had Sommers "barricaded" behind blind-drawn windows. His young son finally looked out and yelled that if reporters didn't stop banging on the door, the police would be called.

After five hours of noise and confusion, watched by neighbours who came out into the street to see what was going on, Sommers' twelve-year-old son, Bob, finally told reporters that his father had decided to talk to them. "My dad says you can come in and to wipe your feet," the boy emphasized. Sommers was apparently keen to keep clean the $607 worth of grey carpeting that was part of his problem.

Sommers looked surprisingly upbeat, healthy, and confident as he turned aside reporters' questions with the polish of a political pro, giving away nothing other than what he wanted to convey. He detailed his medical condition. Sommers said his recurring attacks of rapid, excessive heartbeating could be so bad that on one occasion he had to lie down on a Calgary street. He maintained it was a thirteen-year-old complaint and agreed that the press and the public hadn't heard about it before. He took the opportunity to attack the *Sun* for "outrageous lies" and criticized all the media for its coverage of his "recent actions." One reporter dubbed the session "cryptic evasion." Ever the politician, Sommers didn't admit to anything.

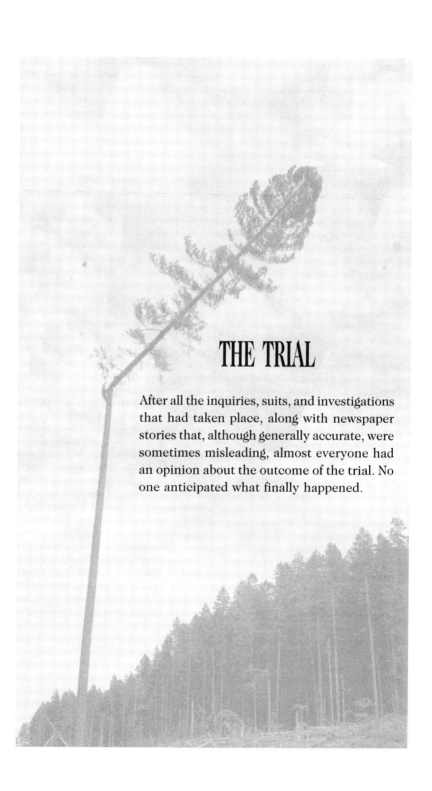

THE TRIAL

After all the inquiries, suits, and investigations that had taken place, along with newspaper stories that, although generally accurate, were sometimes misleading, almost everyone had an opinion about the outcome of the trial. No one anticipated what finally happened.

Sommers' Arrest

Premier Bennett finally realized that the string had run out. There was no point in trying to find new legal angles to stall the process; there was no place for anyone to hide. The government finally acted. On Thursday, November 21, the RCMP, on orders from Attorney General Bonner, arrived at Sommers' house at breakfast time and charged him with bribery and conspiracy. It was 707 days since David Sturdy's first appearance before the original Sloan commission looking into the government's issuing of forest management licences. Since Sturdy launched his attack, Sommers had won an election, lost a libel case, had a contempt charge against Finlayson thrown out of court, and disappeared in the U.S. for two months.

There was no trauma in the Sommers household. A police matron was on hand in case Mrs. Sommers reacted badly. She didn't. Sommers seemed almost relieved and joked with police who flew with him by private plane to Vancouver. Arrested at the same time in Vancouver were Wick Gray and Charlie Schultz. John Gray also was charged, but he was out of town and not picked up until later. Police said other charges were pending. The final phase of the Hundred Years' War had begun, with the bugle at long last sounding the charge. Many fates were now on the line.

For more than two years the people of B.C. had read about the trials and tribulations of the man from Rossland-Trail. Some had expected him to wriggle out again or perhaps remain in the U.S. Then suddenly they read "Sommers Arrested on Bribery Charge." Almost every move was recorded as the former minister arrived in Vancouver too late for a jail breakfast but well in time for lunch. The public was informed that his first meal in prison consisted of corned beef, mashed potatoes, cabbage, carrots, tea, and bread.

Wearing a grey business suit, grey overcoat, and white shirt, but no tie, Sommers made a twenty-minute court appearance with Wick Gray and Charlie Schultz. The room was packed with people eager to share the moment. Magistrate Oscar Orr refused to free Sommers on his own recognizance, noting that he had recently returned from the U.S. and "I'm wondering if his health might not make him go away again." It was an unkind cut, but another lawyer, Nick Mussallem, now acting for Sommers, said there was no chance of that. Sommers nodded agreement from the prisoner's box and made his only utterance when he noted "Yes, that is correct." Former cabinet minister or not,

The beginning of the end came for Sommers on November 21, when police arrived at his Victoria home to arrest him. RCMP officers escorted him to the Vancouver city jail, where he was placed behind bars for the first time.

Orr wasn't taking any chances, and the magistrate stated he "would not even consider allowing Sommers to go free on bail. The charge is too serious and the case is complicated by the fact that Sommers has been away."

After contemplation, however, and a reminder from Mussallem that the accused had returned of his own free will from the south, Orr did set bail at $7,500 for Sommers and $5,000 each for Gray and Schultz. The three were held in a sixteen-bed dormitory until evening, when bail was posted. Neighbours in a larger dormitory across the hall were 60 noisy drunks, also waiting to be processed that day. The judge charged the three men with bribery and conspiracy, although detailed charges would be laid out later. Sommers was in jail exactly eleven hours. Officials said he got no special treatment. Leaving the courthouse, Sommers told reporters, "I am glad to get this right out in the open."

One man pleased with the charge against Sommers was Judge Sloan, who announced with some relief that his royal commission into Sturdy's original charges, which had been adjourned until December 8, was over. He said he was "indeed pleased to be relieved of my duties as commissioner." He had accepted them originally with considerable reluctance and only under pressure from the premier, who recognized the considerable talents of Mr. Justice Sloan. Reporters had been chasing any and all politicians since the charges were laid. They finally caught up with Robert Bonner, who stated, "The charges laid do not encompass all the territory covered in the original allegations. Since the commission appeared to be heading for delay, it was felt this course was the best to ensure the matter proceed." Bonner assured them, "The matter will proceed with dispatch and any motions for delay will be resisted." He noted that Sommers would retain his seat as an MLA and could be disqualified only if he was convicted of a felony or "infamous crime." Bennett had nothing to add to Bonner's statement, and he carefully noted, "These legal matters aren't under me."

Critics were caustic about Bonner's sudden conversion to the need for speed. A *Sun* editorial headline stated "Despite All the Stalling the Law Takes Its Course," and the writer noted, "It took Attorney General Bonner almost two years to realize that you can't fool all the people all the time."

Opposition members said that after running and ducking for so long, the government now appreciated that it was up against the wall and the only strategy remaining was to get the crisis over with as quickly as possible and face the music. Speed, however, was not on the agenda.

At his first court appearance, Charlie Schultz's lawyer, Alfred Bull, feigned amazement when prosecutor Stewart McMorran said he wasn't ready to proceed. The next day the aggressive lawyer seemed genuinely put out when McMorran asked for and received a three-week adjournment because he needed to have discussions with Bonner. Bull was further infuriated by McMorran's request at the next court appearance for another five-week adjournment, noting that more charges were pending. Bull asked for a list of witnesses, copies of statements made, and the RCMP report. McMorran refused, saying they weren't his to give.

Charles Eversfield was not happy with the turn of events and complained that it was costing him $362 a week to stay in town and assist the police with their investigations. He said his wife and son were forced to go to work to keep themselves. Prosecutor McMorran made arrangements for him to be paid $65-a-day living expenses.

The biggest personal tragedy of the affair occurred on December 2, 1957. Early in the day the RCMP went to the office of BCFP president Hector Munro. They questioned the forest company executive about

David Sturdy's allegations that the company was deeply involved in the bribery affair. Munro left his office distraught and near collapse. He died that night. The cause was given as a heart attack, but there was speculation he took his own life, and many of those close to him believed he did. Press reports steered clear of the cause of death.

Munro, aged 52, was described as one of B.C.'s most prominent lumbermen, well known in business and social circles. He had been a favourite of H.R. MacMillan and accompanied him to Ottawa when MacMillan took on a wartime job. Later H.R. asked Munro to take over the management of BCFP, where he was retained as president even after the management contract held by MacMillan ran out and BCFP became an independently operated, Argus-owned company. MacMillan was shaken by the death of his close friend, and his biography makes it clear he knew Munro had taken his own life.

On the day Munro died, a statement that had been issued jointly by BCFP chairman E.P. Taylor and Munro showed the company's annual profit was down $1.9 million from the previous year to a total of $1.02 million. Business was slipping. The company blamed reduced markets, low prices, and the high premium on the Canadian dollar.

To add to the political ferment, Bennett sprang a surprise year-end announcement that Judge Sloan had agreed to quit the bench and become B.C.'s forest czar, charged with cleaning up the industry. The premier announced a whopping $50,000-a-year salary, $20,000 more than Sloan had been making as a judge, and a lot more than Bennett made as premier. It was a ten-year appointment. Bennett said the move would put forestry administration "above and beyond the reach of petty partisan politics." It was a pre-emptive strike, aimed at convincing everyone that no matter what emerged from the Sommers affair, the forestry situation was well in hand. Bennett knew better than anyone else that he must restore confidence in his handling of the province's chief money-maker. The premier said Sloan would have the authority to hold public tribunals on any forestry matter. He maintained the system had been "snarled" in partisanship since the FML system began in 1948, repeating exactly what Gibson and other critics had hammered away at for years, but which the government had denied until now. In effect, Bennett bounced Sloan's own commission recommendations back to him to implement.

The new czar was respected in the forestry community, and his appointment was generally well received by the industry, although a few company leaders questioned some of the recommendations he was about to implement. Sloan received guarded support from labour, which had fears of the growing power of industry, increased mechanization in the woods, and job loss. Liberal leader Art Laing pointed out that it was a new ballgame for the judge. He said Sloan was no longer "blessed with neutrality." Now he was Bennett's politically appointed man.

As the year ran out, Mr. Justice J.V. Clyne announced that he too was quitting the bench but gave no reason why. Many wondered about the resignation, but a week later they learned of Clyne's appointment to the top spot at MacMillan Bloedel Ltd. H.R. later admitted this was a great mistake.

Fateful '58

In early January 1958, detailed counts of conspiracy and 50 charges involving the giving and receiving of bribes were laid against Robert Sommers, Charlie Schultz and his company, Wick Gray and his company, John Gray, Evergreen Lumber Sales, and BCFP. The large forest company's late president Hector Munro was also named in the indictment. His replacement, G.D. Dickey, stated, "It is our intention to defend ourselves against these unjust charges."

Despite the events taking place in court, Nick Mussallem sought permission for Sommers to sit at the upcoming spring session of the legislature. The lawyer explained that his client "represents Rossland-Trail and feels very strongly that he has a public duty towards the people to sit in the House when January 23 arrives and continue throughout the session." Magistrate Orr would have none of it. Sommers then talked to Bennett who, surprisingly, said he wanted him in the House. Arrangements subsequently were made so that Sommers would not have to attend all the preliminary hearing, set to begin on February 12, but he would have to appear if for any reason he was needed in court.

All eyes were on Sommers when he entered the legislative chamber for the new session of parliament on January 23. Not all his colleagues were delighted to see him. He wasn't ostracized, but some backbenchers warily kept their distance. Despite his predicament and clouded future, Sommers was his usual natty, composed self. His presence dominated the opening scene.

There was a nasty clash between Sommers and Victoria Liberal George Gregory. Sarcasm dripped from every word as Gregory

Mel Bryan and W.A.C. Bennett shared a platform during the 1956 election. By early 1958, however, Bryan had crossed the floor to sit as an Independent, claiming Bonner should have acted sooner to investigate the charges against Sommers. Bennett called him a traitor and a "Liberal plant."

congratulated Sommers on the apparent recovery of his health. From his backbench seat Sommers, eyes blazing, fought back. He said Gregory was "yellow" and had no guts. Gregory's face went pale with anger, but he didn't retaliate.

In the tense, smouldering atmosphere it wasn't long before the Sommers affair again burst into flame. The first crack in what had been a solid Socred front split wide open when North Vancouver MLA Mel Bryan, a local newspaper publisher elected in 1956, stood up and shocked his colleagues by demanding Bonner's resignation. Only a week into the session, the 45-year-old rookie member brought silence to the House as he condemned Bonner for having done nothing for two-and-a-half years and having failed in his duty. Bonner was stunned by the assault and listened tight-lipped as the rebel Socred accused him of lacking "appreciation of the basic concepts relevant to the high office he holds." Bryan told the House he was not prepared to sacrifice principle for party unity and added, "It is a fundamental issue that should have been dealt with without any concern for political considerations and party loyalties." The rookie said he became a candidate on assurances from Bonner "that there was more sound and fury than substance in the allegations" concerning Sommers. He had been told they were "far-fetched."

Bonner hit back. "I have never walked away from a tough job in my life and I don't intend to start now," he told reporters.

Bennett was not in the house. He was in Vancouver attending a planning meeting for the Queen Mother's upcoming visit to B.C. When reporters confronted him, the unruffled premier came to Bonner's defence, sparing none of his superlatives, stating Bonner was "the most outstanding attorney general this province or any other province has ever had." He lashed out at his favourite target, the newspapers, angrily claiming they made "headlines over nothing, playing up little things."

A caucus meeting was called in Victoria, and while neither Bennett nor Bonner were in attendance, it was obvious the caucus listened to their instructions. They decided not to kick Bryan out and make a martyr of him, but rather to isolate him. Asked later if he had asked Bryan to quit the party, Bennett retorted that he never asked people to leave Social Credit—"I only ask them to join."

Bonner was less sanguine. He was aware that at least six caucus members quietly supported Bryan and shared his opinion that Bonner had bobbled the Sommers strategy, although they publicly voiced the view that there was no need for Bonner to resign. The views of these Socred backbenchers, as much as anything Bennett or Bonner said, possibly swayed the caucus to let Bryan stay.

It was a field day for the opposition, which invited Bryan to cross the floor as Bennett had done when he walked away from the Coalition government seven years earlier. The pressure even brought a surprising statement from a usually compliant Socred backbencher, John Tisdalle. He went so far as to say, "I am not admitting the attorney general erred, but if he did he should be treated with understanding and forgiveness." With friends like this, Bonner didn't need enemies.

On February 4 a tense Bryan rose again in the House and said he had been naive to believe the government would take notice of his remarks. They had been greeted with nothing but a deafening silence. "I have no illusions about leading a revolt, but I know my feelings on this issue are shared by others on this side of the House. It was at

James K. Nesbitt joined the legislative press gallery in 1936 and filed copy during the reigns of six premiers: Pattullo, Hart, Johnson, Bennett, Barrett, and Bill Bennett. He started off with the Victoria Times, *but for many years was the Victoria correspondent for the* Vancouver Sun.

their urging on Wednesday that I did not cross the floor. They said publicly that they thought my timing was wrong," stated the rebel newspaper publisher turned politician.

Times had changed. Pandemonium broke out as Bryan moved from behind his desk, walked across the floor, and took a seat on the opposition side behind Gregory. Socreds jeered and the opposition cheered. Bennett was beside himself with rage, yelling, "Traitor, traitor." Seeming to lose his cool, the premier succumbed to political paranoia, contending that Bryan was never a Socred but actually a Liberal plant, and that he had packed his nomination meeting with friends to worm his way in. Like storms from the Pacific that often lash Victoria and then quickly die away, the affair subsided.

Two days after the mini-revolt, Sommers made a speech in the legislature. Columnist James K. Nesbitt reported, "He talked well, humorously, in perfect control of himself, sparring just a bit with the opposition, praising the government, but suggesting now and then that the government could improve things. There was no trace of bitterness about him, no crying, just a forthright, pleasantly delivered speech from the backbencher."

Bennett led the applause both before and after Sommers spoke. The opposition obviously agreed to listen quietly and, for the public's benefit, not kick a man when he was down. The former minister told the House that he didn't mind the sniping he had suffered at the hands of the opposition over such a long time. Sommers said he was reminded of an old French proverb that stated people only throw stones at trees laden with fruit. The opposition had to think about that one.

Sommers talked about his riding, its development, and its needs. For a man who was going to depend on them a lot, he took a surprising swipe at lawyers. He said they only wanted a new Vancouver courthouse with more room so they could make more money. In the next few months Sommers would have plenty of opportunity to assess the accommodation in the courthouse, to identify its needs, and to observe the legal profession.

The Preliminary Trial Begins

The excitement and curiosity engendered in the public by more than two years of accusations, rumours, and news stories brought out a standing-room-only crowd when the preliminary hearing opened in Vancouver on February 12.

Magistrate Orr had requested Sommers be in attendance, and his appearance dramatically emphasized how quickly he had fallen, from the corridors of power and prestige to the prisoners' box. With him in the dock were the three other accused: Charlie Schultz, Wick Gray, and John Gray. Sommers told the court that he elected to be tried by a judge and jury. The other three followed suit. Not-guilty pleas were entered to all charges against the four men and the listed companies involved. Prosecutor McMorran said there would be 40 witnesses and 720 documents entered as exhibits.

The first witness was Trevor Daniels, a former chief financial officer for BCFP. He said he was sent to Vancouver by E.P. Taylor and was employed by BCFP from 1946 until he quit late in 1954. He contended that the company's move to obtain an FML led to the bribery of Sommers. As spectators in the crowded courtroom hung on every word, Daniels testified that the late BCFP president Hector Munro had told him a deal had been made in Toronto for the company to obtain its licence, and $30,000 had been allocated to get it through Sommers. Munro told Daniels the money was to go through Wick Gray, with "part or all of it to go to Mr. Sommers." He said he quit the company after a "tremendous verbal row" with Munro over this arrangement. He testified he told the president that it was "extremely foolish."

From his own knowledge as treasurer of the company, Daniels said a $15,000 cheque had been given to Pacific Coast Services and charged to the engineering and cruising account of BCFP's central logging division. It was followed by another $15,000 cheque. At the time of the transaction, the ex-financial officer said, Munro claimed it was a bona fide transaction, although Daniels knew of no actual cruising or engineering work done for BCFP by PCS. Munro had also told Daniels to cash a $2,500 cheque for Sommers and his family when they went east, the money to be given to Wick Gray and billed as a political donation to the Socreds.

When prosecutor McMorran asked about his relationship with the BCFP president, Daniels denied hating Munro and wanting his job, pointing out that they frequently were seen together socially. He said he never wanted to be company president and bore no resentment that he didn't get the position.

Findlay S. McKinnon, B.C.'s assistant chief forester, took the stand, and in answer to a question from the prosecution testified that Sommers personally negotiated the BCFP application for FML #22. McKinnon testified, "In the case of this application, the negotiations and almost all of the discussion was carried on by the minister and the applicant." Normal procedure was for an applicant to come to department officials for discussions. "They would negotiate with the forest service first and not the minister." In the BCFP case, a letter regarding FML #22 arrived in Victoria on January 24, 1955, signed by Hector Munro. McKinnon said Sommers ordered a report on it to be on his desk in two days. "He told me very plainly he didn't want an eight- or ten- or twelve-page report telling how this could not be done, what he wanted was a one-page report on how it could be done," he testified. McKinnon said Sommers also told him, "If the forest service could not come up with an idea as to how it could be done he would have to go outside the service to find someone who could do it." The treatment obviously still rankled McKinnon. He told the court that he had "never before been spoken to in that manner."

Another witness was Dr. C.D. Orchard, the long-time chief forester and deputy minister of the department, which he held under a tight rein. Regarded as dogmatic and dictatorial by many who served under him, he had few friends among his subordinates. Both Sommers and his successor, Ray Williston, had difficulty dealing with him. Williston described Orchard, a keen advocate of the FML system, as a man who was unable to deal effectively with many of the more controversial problems that arose in his department, preferring to delegate any nasty duties to his subordinates. A dry, humourless man, he had knitted together a centralized, inflexible department, which was totally revamped when Williston took over and Orchard retired. Orchard had said next to nothing at the brief Lord Commission, perhaps for fear of losing his job. Now he told the court that Bennett had made the final decision on granting BCFP its licence. Orchard said Sommers took him to a meeting in the premier's office on May 14. There were only the three people present. "The decision was given to me," Dr. Orchard testified. "I suppose the premier was given the decision by the minister. I just stood there and listened," he added. The witness said he disapproved of the deal because BCFP would be allowed to overcut. "I was absolutely and fundamentally against it," he stressed, but he had kept quiet until now.

An odd witness with a stranger story was W.D. Samson, an army paratrooper and Sommers' brother-in-law. In 1954 he was working for the forest service when his foreman told him to drive Sommers and his wife on a trip north. Samson said that he asked Sommers for a loan, and Sommers phoned Schultz in Vancouver to arrange a $500 loan for him. Some wondered why Samson had not gone directly to the department if this was expense money needed for the trip north on official forest business, but perhaps Samson, knowing that Orchard was at odds with Sommers, preferred to submit the expense account with all receipts attached rather than seeking an advance from the department for a trip involving the minister. Samson said the money was wired to Dawson Creek and he turned it over to Sommers for "safekeeping." He added that the loan was later repaid.

The linchpin in the case, Charles Eversfield, took the stand and was first asked about his personal history. He said he was born in Alberta in 1911, came to B.C. in the 1920s, worked in Vancouver shipyards during the Second World War, and then began his own bookkeeping business. He went to work for Wick Gray and PCS in 1951. Eversfield quickly asserted that he only "carried out instructions" in the transactions of the company. He added that when he first went to see David Sturdy, the lawyer told him that he had been acting as an agent for an employer and had committed no wrongdoing. Eversfield confirmed earlier testimony about the financial juggling and transfers of money to Sommers. He testified he sent Sommers a $2,500 cheque, four $500 bonds, and $1,000 in cash through the mail. He said that PCS had also picked up the $607 tab for Sommers' East Indian rugs. The prosecution later said the cartage van that delivered the rugs from the store to Victoria had been tracked and PCS had paid by cheque.

John Nicholson, now the lawyer for PCS, launched the first of many verbal attacks made on Eversfield during the next few months. It was a savage assault aimed at destroying the accountant's credibility. Nicholson accused him of trying to shake down Wick Gray for $10,000. Eversfield denied any blackmail attempt.

The confusing complexity of the charges became increasingly evident as Eversfield explained the many transactions involving Sommers, Wick Gray, Charlie Schultz, and BCFP. Document after document was identified and introduced as evidence, along with information about the peculiar forms of transfer used to get money to Sommers in Victoria.

S.H. Armitage, a vice-president of PCS, provided further information on Wick Gray's companies. He testified that in the summer of 1954 the company finances were in such bad shape that voluntary liquidation was being considered. They had, however, recovered somewhat since then. He also identified Wick Gray as a "rabid Socred," someone who would do almost anything to help the party stay in power. That generally meant obtaining more funds from members for party coffers.

Thora Peterson, personal secretary to Charlie Schultz from 1951 to 1954, told the hearing that when the Lord Commission investigating Gibson's money-talks allegations was announced, she was told to take six files and five letters out of the company files. They included the BCFP file and Schultz's own personal files. Peterson said the letters all dealt with various FML applications. Bull, representing Schultz, fought to have her testimony disallowed, but lost. Peterson, described by the papers as tall and fair, said Schultz told her the material concerned the BCFP licence application and he wanted it "out of circulation." The witness said she took the material home, kept it there for a week, and then returned it to the office after the three-day Lord Commission ended. Ms. Peterson also testified that Schultz's company did a lot more work on FMLs after Sommers became minister than it did before he took the post.

Another accountant called by the prosecution as a preliminary witness was George Davenport, a former accountant with C.D. Schultz, who testified that there had been items "altered or obliterated" in the company's ledgers.

On March 6, Magistrate Oscar Orr committed the accused for trial. Bail was hiked to $10,000 each for the three major accused and $6,000 for John Gray. Bull contended that Eversfield was an accomplice; he had been involved in devious transactions to hide the transfer of funds and should not be allowed to go back to the U.S., but

Cyril Shelford, MLA for Omineca, was a longtime backbencher, not afraid to speak out when he disagreed with Socred policy or direction. He was convinced that his criticism of Bonner's handling of the Sommers affair kept him out of Bennett's cabinet until he was finally named minister of agriculture in 1968.

the magistrate disagreed. When BCFP was ordered to stand trial four days later, lawyer Walter Owen said he would not attempt to have the charge thrown out because without a trial "there may be in some minds imputations which could be wrong." He added that because the company was not charged until after president Munro died, there were now "considerable handicaps" for himself and BCFP.

While both sides waited for the trial date, the opposition turned the heat up on Bonner in the legislature. CCF leader Bob Strachan moved a no-confidence motion, maintaining that for almost two years there was "deliberate evasion and failure to act." The government easily beat the motion by a 29 to 14 vote, but in a significant development, three Socred backbenchers (Cyril Shelford, Irvine Corbett, and Fred Sharp) quietly slipped away to avoid voting. Their defection was widely reported by the media.

The bruising and bitter legislative session ended March 20, with the government bandaging its wounds. Bennett as always put on his happy face, crowing about his government's accomplishments. The next day a meeting of legal representatives in the Vancouver courthouse set a trial date of May 1. Veteran lawyer Victor Dryer would be prosecutor, with Stewart McMorran his assistant.

Sun gossip columnist Jack Wasserman wondered whether "Premier Bennett would be called as a witness for the defence." Wasserman was more often right than wrong, but the public appreciated that Bennett in the witness box would be something for the books. Was the premier prepared to undergo examination and cross-examination of his handling of the Sommers affair? The political pros said Bennett wouldn't testify even to save Sommers' skin unless he was summonsed. The press and the public waited.

The Sommers Trial

As Bob Sommers awaited his trial, political developments at the federal level put a crimp in the national dreams of the Social Credit Party. At the end of March 1958, Progressive Conservative rookie Prime Minister John Diefenbaker scored the greatest victory in Canadian federal political history. There were parallels with Bennett's own rise to power. In the general election that followed Diefenbaker's months-old minority government's defeat in the legislature, he took his party from 112 to 208 seats, basically on his own charisma. The Liberals were demolished, falling to 49 seats from 105. Social Credit was annihilated, all nineteen members swept out by the coast-to-coast juggernaut. In B.C. the Liberals lost their only two seats and the CCF dropped from seven to four. The triumphant Tories took eighteen seats in B.C., compared to seven they had held previously. One of these seats went to Douglas Jung, the first Chinese-Canadian ever elected to a Canadian parliament.

British Columbians were still learning to live with the new Canadian political picture when the curtain finally rose on the Sommers trial in Vancouver's stately old courthouse on Georgia Street (now the site of the Vancouver Art Gallery) on May 1. The public had read much about Sommers in the preceding years and didn't know what to believe. They were particularly fascinated by the details of the evidence exposed for the first time at the preliminary hearing. Complex money transactions, the involvement of top business people in Vancouver and Toronto, and the various cover-up attempts held their attention.

The public seats were crowded when Chief Justice J.O. Wilson sat down on the bench and opened the proceedings. Many lawyers had been surprised at his appointment as presiding judge because he had been particularly caustic and critical of Robert Sommers when he tossed out the MLA's libel suit against David Sturdy.

Included in the line-up for the defence were some of Vancouver's most prestigious lawyers. Representing Bob Sommers was Angelo Branca, one of the city's best-known criminal lawyers, who later said he never knew who actually paid his hefty bill. Douglas McK. Brown

The architecture of the Vancouver courthouse, opened in 1911, was intended to convey the pomp and seriousness of the legal system. Less than two months before his trial began, Robert Sommers criticized lawyers who were calling for a new, bigger courthouse. He had plenty of time over the summer of 1958 to gauge the building's adequacy.

was counsel for BCFP, and Alfred Bull represented Charlie Schultz and his company. Defending Wick Gray and PCS was J.R. Nicholson. E.E. Hinkson defended John Gray.

The defence lawyers set the stage for what was to come when they complained that seventeen new charges, the details of which filled fourteen typewritten pages, had been delivered to them only the previous night. Alfred Bull said an RCMP officer had brought the documents to his home at 10 p.m. Prosecutor Dryer explained that the new material repeated the substance of the earlier charges but in much more detail. Judge Wilson agreed, however, to adjourn until May 6 to give defence attorneys an opportunity to consider the new documents. The judge said the lateness of the new charges was "most regrettable and lamentable," but he felt there was no suggestion that the Crown had been unfair.

On May 6 the judge dismissed a defence appeal to kill 28 of the charges, but there was to be another delay. Accused John Gray was obviously unwell, diagnosed with flu, and Wilson called for a second adjournment until May 12. These and later recesses and adjournments were to produce the longest trial to that time in B.C. history. It was delayed at least five times—once for a month—by the sickness of a juror, one of the accused, or one of the lawyers. The jury sat for 83 days in all, spread over more than six headline-making months.

It also was one of the most complicated trials in the province's history. Much of the evidence was in the avalanche of more than 1000 documents that were presented during the case. They led the jurors through bewildering, twisting trails of devious money transactions, altered accounts, and phoney receipts. A handcart was needed to move the mounting pile of papers in and out of the courtroom. At the outset there were two conspiracy charges and 30 charges of giving and accepting bribes, down from the original 50, although the number was reduced even further during the proceedings.

Sorting out the many charges, the motions to dismiss, the complex legal arguments, and the confusing web of dates and amounts of money involved was a monumental task for Justice Wilson and the twelve men and women of the jury, in whose hands lay the fate of the accused. Despite massive, and generally accurate, media coverage, the public at times had difficulty in determining exactly who did what to whom. The lawyers cited arcane points of law, dug into ancient English history, and made sweeping allegations. One assertion was that the entire affair was a Liberal plot to bring down Bennett's government. Defence arguments, in a nutshell, contended that any monies Sommers may have received were either political donations to the party or personal loans that were not bribes for ministerial favours.

The trial took place during a heat wave, severe by Vancouver standards, so it wasn't only the accused who sweated it out in the old, non-air-conditioned courthouse. It took only 43 minutes to pick a jury of three women and nine men from the 112 people who were selected for possible duty. Halfway through the swearing in, one potential juror stopped and blurted out, "I cannot go on with this. I feel I am prejudiced." He was replaced, and he was lucky. Judge Wilson told the twelve selected that he would not have them locked up for the duration of the trial because it would create too much of a personal hardship. At that time he had no idea of the length of the marathon that was beginning, but he knew it would not be short.

Two hundred pleas of not guilty were entered in just fifteen minutes, one of the few fast aspects of the case. Judge Wilson refused defence pleas to have another thirteen of the charges dropped and also rejected submissions that there be separate trials for the conspiracy and the bribery charges.

The defence lawyers argued at some length that the Parliament of Canada had made a mistake in drafting the relevant part of the Canadian Criminal Code. They maintained that while it was an offence to bribe a minister, the code did not state that it was an offence for a minister to accept a bribe. Judge Wilson commented that whoever drafted the bill might have missed a few points, but at the moment he was not throwing out anything because of this argument. It was a point that would resurface later in the trial.

Each juror received a loose-leaf folder and photostats of more than 700 documents. It took three days for the prosecution to introduce them. The long, drawn-out procedure brought the jury foreman Eric Miller to his feet, asking plaintively, "Is it necessary for us to go through this ordeal?" The answer from the bench was a succinct "Yes."

It was only the first of many travails for the jurors over the following months. As the documents and papers entered in evidence piled up, Judge Wilson commented that he hoped for his and the jury's sake there would soon be a "lecture on bookkeeping" because of the complexity of the papers being introduced. When defence lawyers clashed on the question of hearsay evidence, Wilson advised them to meet and sort out their differences. With much of Vancouver's top legal talent involved, there was more than a little temperament in the courtroom.

The atmosphere in court became even more dramatic when prosecutor Stewart McMorran called Charles Eversfield to the witness box. His testimony was electrifying as he identified numerous PCS receipts for entertaining Sommers. When he noted a receipt for champagne, Bull sarcastically commented to McMorran, "And don't forget the ginger ale." Eversfield said he sent money to Sommers, but refused to make out a $1,200 cheque for himself that was supposedly a salary bonus but actually was to be additional money for Sommers. He recalled seeing Wick Gray stuffing bills in a wallet, slapping it, and saying, "That should make Bob happy." Eversfield contended he was an accountant carrying out orders and was not actively involved in what he began to realize were a series of unlawful undertakings. There was some excited murmuring in the public gallery when the accountant described a document he said Wick Gray ordered him to prepare. It listed monies received, monies promised, and monies expected up to the end of November 1954 from companies wanting FMLs. Eversfield said his calculations based on these figures showed Sommers would receive $48,960—his split of an anticipated $193,000 total. The accountant said $20,000 of Sommers' take would come from a total of $80,000 received from BCFP. He told the court he kept these documents about FMLs away from other company records.

J.R. Nicholson, lawyer for Wick Gray, questioned Eversfield very closely and then accused him of blackmail. Eversfield admitted he asked for compensation before leaving PCS because he had not been paid what had been promised. He denied demanding $10,000 or a share in the business. Eversfield said PCS was in such tough shape that it would have been a losing proposition anyway. He didn't wilt under the heaviest attack, and the public seemed sympathetic as he withstood the assault. When he corrected one of the defence lawyers for a minor mistake in recounting evidence, Eversfield got a round of applause from the public galleries, which resulted in a threat from Wilson to clear the courtroom. Eversfield recounted that when the government ordered the short-lived Lord Commission, Gray had stated, "If I go down, everyone goes down with me." Gray, he added, emphasized "everyone." Eversfield had a tough ten days in the box, but seldom faltered, nor did the defence catch him giving any significant contradictory or damaging answers. He had a jaunty walk as he left the witness stand, flashing a smile to reporters, some of whom he had come to know well.

When he took the stand at the trial, Trevor Daniels, the former BCFP chief financial officer, again told about his argument with company president Hector Munro, giving more details than he had at the preliminary hearing. The former top executive testified that he had told Munro that agreeing to a $30,000 deal, most of which was to be passed to Sommers, "was a very foolish thing to do." He added, "I told Mr. Munro that I wasn't satisfied that the business with PCS was on the level and that possibly the same situation existed with C.D. Schultz. I resented being involved. We had a most unfortunate altercation." Daniels then gave notice of his resignation from BCFP.

Daniels explained that the next day Munro asked for his help. "He had thought things over and came to the conclusion that he had got himself into a great deal of difficulty," Daniels stated. His evidence was allowed, although the defence protested that Munro was not there to defend himself.

Alfred Bull exploded when the former BCFP employee referred to "gossip" he heard on the street about the company's FML application. The lawyer said he would demand a new trial if there was an attempt to introduce any more hearsay evidence. Bull then grilled Daniels, trying to show that his testimony came from a disgruntled, unhappy man who had been passed over for BCFP's top job. Daniels stood by his statements without hesitation. He caused a stir in the public benches, however, when he told the court that he continued to receive $10,000 annually from BCFP. Asked if it was a pension, he replied that it was "more in the form of a retainer, I think."

Daniels had been brought to Vancouver by E.P. Taylor to take over a senior position at BCFP. It was never verified whether he had been promised the president's job or not. He gave the impression he was an insider who knew what was going on and who got out as soon as he smelled more trouble than he was prepared to handle.

The jury and the spectators got a first-hand look at the world of high finance, big-business thinking, and its attendant lifestyle in Toronto when bluff, gruff-voiced Wallace McCutcheon took the stand. He was E.P. Taylor's right-hand man, a vice-president of Argus, and a major financial figure, one of the tea sippers when Sommers visited Taylor's home. Well dressed, confident, and arrogant, McCutcheon typified executive thinking at the corporation; what was good for Argus was obviously good for Canada.

McCutcheon denied asking Trevor Daniels, at the height of the Sommers crisis, if BCFP was "now in the clear." He related the details of a strange hotel-room meeting with Daniels, however, which took place when he came to Vancouver in December 1957 for Munro's funeral. McCutcheon said Daniels had asked him if he knew about the involvement of the company with forests minister Robert Sommers. "He closed the doors, pledged me to secrecy, and asked if I wanted to know. I was about to go to a funeral and I wasn't interested in hearing what he had to say so I said no," McCutcheon related. His response could have made jurors wonder if his lack of interest was because he already knew what had been going on. He seemed too gruff, too confident, and appeared to dismiss much of his own testimony as of minor importance, too insignificant for serious consideration.

McCutcheon laughed at suggestions that Gray's hotel bill in Toronto seemed high if it was only for one person. He said he wouldn't give it a thought and added, "My own bill is running higher." A $2,500 payment to Wick Gray wasn't much, he said. "It depends on how he entertains." Asked if he thought Gray was casual in running up big taxi bills, McCutcheon said he didn't think so. In a money-really-doesn't-matter vein, he noted that on occasion he had kept taxi meters running for up to five hours waiting for him.

When referring to the Victoria meeting with Bennett and Sommers to discuss the new FML application, which he attended with E.P. Taylor in the Empress Hotel, McCutcheon told the court that Bennett, Sommers, and the others who were present—Bonner, Ralph Chetwynd, and Ken Kiernan—seemed receptive to their proposals. He underlined that Bennett called the shots, and recalled the premier said to go ahead and work out the details with Sommers and his staff. E.P. Taylor was not called to appear as a witness at the trial.

On June 23, Judge Wilson provided the court with a new complication. He said the charges had been laid under section 102 of the new Criminal Code, but the alleged offences had taken place in 1954, before the new code came into effect. The old law stated that a charge must be laid within two years; the new law did not. The judge decided the old law no longer applied and the case would be tried under the new law. Carefully spreading the blame without fingering anyone in particular, Wilson said it was unfortunate that this matter had not occurred to him earlier. He added, however, that he would be doing himself an injustice "if I omitted to say that the point had not occurred to any of the talented gentlemen of this bar now before me." The judge said the oversight had "very serious implications."

The defence had missed the crucial point in the relative dates in the Criminal Code, but it now tried to use the information provided by the judge to its advantage. When the prosecution closed its case on June 24, defence lawyers leapt to their feet in a bid to have all charges dismissed, but Judge Wilson ruled the trial must proceed under the new code. There had to this point been 45 witnesses and 3,000 pages of evidence recorded over 30 days.

Judge Wilson then ordered thirteen charges against Sommers be dropped on various technical points ranging from improper language to insufficient information. He threw out one of the conspiracy charges for similar reasons. A legal donnybrook ensued as defence lawyers once again sought to have all charges dismissed. The jury, already reeling from the confusion produced by accounting allegations and the hundreds of documents tabled, was spared having to listen to the legal battle. Judge Wilson excused them for an initial four days, which was later extended, although he did try to explain to them on recall what had happened during their absence. It wasn't easy. Much of the four-day discussion centred on the argument raised earlier as to whether a minister was an official. According to the code, it was an offence to bribe an official, but the code did not state whether it was an offence for a minister or an official to accept a bribe. At one point, Nicholson went back to thirteenth-century English common law, also citing cases from the reigns of Edward I and King Henry VIII and what was said to the Archbishop of Canterbury on occasion. Nicholson didn't win. On June 27, Judge Wilson ruled that a minister was also an official. Adjourning the court for five days, the judge said he was "quite relieved for the rest. I have been having my troubles lately."

As the court adjourned for the day on July 8, Judge Wilson commented that there was "a nightmare of complexities." He had the full agreement of the jurors and the public who had been trying to follow the legalities of the case but were having some difficulty. At one point he wearily sighed, "There are so many motions that I have lost count."

The following day the judge tossed out another five bribery charges against Sommers for lack of direct evidence. As the dust settled, the defence began to mount its case. The offences were down to one charge of conspiracy and a total of nineteen counts of bribery facing all the accused. Sommers faced the conspiracy charge and seven counts of accepting bribes, while Gray faced one charge of conspiracy and eight counts of giving bribes. Charges also remained against Pacific Coast Services for conspiracy and bribery, and against Evergreen Services, Charlie Schultz and his company, C.D. Schultz and Associates, John Gray, and BCFP for bribery.

Some of Judge Wilson's problems with the case were explained when he announced in the courtroom, to the astonishment of those in attendance, that he had been receiving "fanatical poison pen letters" claiming that he was on the side of the accused. He said he was only doing his duty and expressed sympathy for the jury and their task. "I know that you are not some of those fanatical people who have been writing to me anonymous letters and have all through this trial, people who accuse me of attempts to free the accused," added Judge Wilson.

Bull jumped on the issue of the letters sent to Judge Wilson, calling it an "organized inspired propaganda movement against the accused."

Wilson dismissed the idea, but told the jurors to let him know if they received any letters "from people on the lunatic fringe." They didn't.

There was a minor revolt when jurors objected to the heat in the courtroom. With the five courtroom doors open in an attempt to beat the heat wave, the temperature remained at 83 degrees Fahrenheit. When male jurors appeared one day in shirtsleeves, Judge Wilson, usually a stickler for decorum, got the message. After the first break he appeared without his wig and gown and told the accused they could take off their jackets.

The atmosphere should have become more relaxed, but it didn't. In fact it became more intense as the defence witnesses took the stand for the first time. This was what everyone had been waiting for. It began simply enough with the testimony of John Gray, aged 47, the older brother of Wick Gray.

During his testimony he made an effort to capitalize on his wartime airforce record, which was a good one. A bomber pilot, he won the Distinguished Flying Cross. Gray said he considered six or seven people at PCS "like a bomber crew with the life and welfare of each individual dependent on the faith and trust of the others." His hand on a bible, he testified that he had been brought up "on the teachings of the Great Teacher in the world." Gray claimed Eversfield had hoodwinked him. He said his brother Wick had told him about money he had collected for Social Credit Party funds and also admitted making personal loans to Sommers. He contended that he had heard Eversfield making blackmail threats to his brother. It was obvious that he was only a bit player, his evidence was unconvincing, and he was of little help to his brother.

When Charlie Schultz took the stand, his lawyer, Alfred Bull, said his client was a ruined man because of this affair. His company, which had been the largest forest consulting firm in Canada, had collapsed from a staff of a hundred to three, and there was now practically no income, from a high of $606,000 in 1956.

A subdued Schultz, 54, the son of a judge, claimed he had hired Wick Gray to do public relations work for him in 1953, despite the fact Gray had no experience in that business. Nevertheless, Gray had contacts, was in touch with influential people, and went to Victoria on Schultz's behalf. He admitted there was nothing in writing and no contract to cover what Gray was supposed to do or what he was to be paid. He was hired on an "old-friend basis." Schultz said he loaned Gray $22,000 in 1953, strictly on his word, with no IOU or written agreement. He told the court that he was repaid $23,000 without any difficulty. Schultz denied being part of any conspiracy and claimed that money paid to Gray was either for work performed or contributions intended for the Socreds. Under cross-examination he stuck to his story. The smiling Schultz seemed hardly concerned about appearing before the court, although some of the evidence against him was very strong. The courtroom environment was familiar to him and he appeared completely at ease, as though his comments were well rehearsed.

The media continued to give massive coverage to the trial, desperately trying to sort out and explain to readers, listeners, and viewers the legal complications, the convoluted arguments, and the mass of conflicting evidence. The Sommers affair had provoked a heated public debate. Everyone had an opinion and many became emotionally involved. On the one side, Socred supporters felt the whole case was a fabrication dreamt up by the Liberals, while Liberal supporters were sure this new fanatical group calling itself the Social Credit Party was out to destroy the country.

In spite of the public debate, during the Grays' and Schultz's testimony there were empty seats in the courtroom caused by flagging public interest and the stifling temperatures. They were filled again on August 7 when Bob Sommers appeared at last to defend himself.

Sommers Tells His Story

Robert Sommers was obviously not bothered by his heart condition when he took the stand. He was calm and confident as always. Lawyer Nick Mussallem, working with Angelo Branca on the defence, described Sommers as a "poor but honest man," a simple schoolteacher suddenly in high office, to which he had been appointed with dignity. Mussallem predicted that Sommers would emerge from the ordeal as a "super salesman for B.C."

It was Day 55 of the trial when Sommers told the jury that in 1952 he had been principal of Castlegar Elementary School, organizer of the local Canadian Legion, president of the Kiwanis Club, and manager of a choir. He first met Wick Gray when a "teacher's pay was so bad you had to have another job and I ran a six-piece orchestra and sold life insurance." Gray hired the band to play at an event he hosted to celebrate the purchase of the Big Bend Lumber Company.

After becoming minister of lands and forests, Sommers said he was approached by Hector Munro, who diplomatically inquired why forestry officials had been so hostile to BCFP's first application for a FML. Sommers checked with the department and found that officials believed BCFP was a cut-and-run operator. He told the court that Munro seemed shocked to hear this. Sommers advised the company president that a future application might succeed if the company developed a plan that would use more small contractors and if BCFP made a capital investment in something like a mill.

Sommers then explained his financial difficulties in Victoria and how he came to borrow money from his only friend on the coast. He detailed monies he received from Gray. There was $2,500 telegraphed to him in Victoria in December 1953. A second loan of $1,000 cash came in January 1954 by registered mail. A third payment of $2,000 was made up of four $500 bonds, which Gray handed to him in February 1954. Sommers added that a fourth loan of $1,000 was received in May 1954 so he could buy a car. The odd ways in which the money was transferred made the transactions appear suspicious. Why were innocent loans not made simply by cheque?

Sommers testified that Gray had come to him when the Lord Commission was appointed and suggested he sign notes for the money he had received. Sommers hadn't signed anything previously because Gray had told him, "I always operate my business on the basis that a man's signature is no better than his word." Sommers went to Bonner after Gray talked to him. Sommers said that on the attorney general's advice, he got a bank loan and paid off the notes.

Sommers' counsel, Angelo Branca, knew the bank loan was a key element in the case, one the jury would wonder about, so he framed his questions to the defendant carefully:

> Branca: "Who knew you had taken out this $8,000 loan?"
> Sommers: "Only three people: The Honourable Premier Bennett, Attorney General Bonner, and Mr. Einar Gunderson."
> Branca: "And it is paid off?"
> Sommers: "Yes."
> Branca: "Who paid it off?"
> Sommers: "I don't know. Three days before these proceedings I stopped at my bank in Victoria and enquired of the bank manager how the loan stood. He told me there was no loan outstanding at the bank. He said he received instructions to forward all data from the bank to the main branch in Vancouver and he said he didn't know who paid it off. I made enquiries but they wouldn't tell me."

Skepticism showed on the faces of the jury and those in the galleries. They found the explanation more than a little suspect and came to their own conclusions as to who would have paid it off. Few of them would ever have been lucky enough to have a mysterious benefactor show up and pay off a loan. No one knew better than Branca that it was a sticky point. He later told the jury, when summing up, "Don't hold that against us. It has no relevancy in this case." (Long after the trial there were unconfirmed reports that the money had come from a Socred slush fund operated by Gunderson.)

Sommers explained his trip east for his daughter's wedding in Detroit, saying that Gray was the only person from the West Coast invited to the event. The jury seemed unconvinced when Sommers maintained that at the time he didn't know Gray was working for Schultz. Sommers admitted he found out later that his hotel bill during the Toronto trip had been paid by BCFP because the company believed it was part of Gray's costs. The minister said this resulted from confusion at the hotel front desk when Gray paid the bill for both of them without telling Sommers about it. "I did not pay the bill when I left, because when I have stayed at Canadian National or Canadian Pacific in the past and have identified myself, they have sent the bill on later. I did not know BCFP was paying," he added. (This may have been a plausible excuse as public servants were, and often still are, billed at lower rates than average travellers through arrangements for volume discounts.)

Over a period of three days, Sommers stood in the dock, telling his story, answering questions from his legal counsel. He used expressive hand gestures and spoke with confidence. During cross-examination, however, Sommers' happy face dissolved. He began easily and could still show flashes of his old style. He drew laughter when Vic Dryer asked him about his bank account. The prosecutor cited one month when the record showed a $1,573 credit balance. Sommers wryly commented, "That must have been one of my better months." Then his memory began to fail him and he became confused about details. Even his wife, watching from the public gallery, seemed shocked, and Sommers turned pale, when Dryer hauled out bank records to show that Sommers had assets of more than $10,000 at the time he maintained he was forced to accept loans from Wick Gray because of shaky personal finances. Dryer produced several documents showing Sommers' assets included $2,000 cash; an insurance policy with a surrender value of $500; a lot in the Interior worth $1,100;

credit in the teachers' superannuation fund of $3,000; and a bank-approved overdraft of $1,000. As Dryer read the records, Sommers stated that he "could not recall giving such details" to the bank manager and didn't remember all of his conversations with him.

Sommers denied any improprieties, contending the money received was personal loans and had no bearing on the granting of FMLs or his other responsibilities as a minister, but the longer he was in the box, the weaker his story became. He was vague about the subject of conversations during some of his dealings with Wick Gray and frequently stated that he couldn't recall the date, the time of day, or the locations of their meetings. At one point during one of his lapses about details and dates, Judge Wilson asked, "You're surely willing to concede that Christmas in 1955 fell on December 25?" Laughter from the jury and the public almost drowned out Sommers' "Yes, My Lord." Wilson's brief, pointed observation capsulized the jury's thinking.

Sommers had a brief recovery, and the public benches were smiling again, when he gave his account of the $500 loan which his brother-in-law, forest department employee W.D. Samson, requested during their trip north. The minister revealed that it was a personal loan for Samson and had nothing to do with business. He said Samson pestered him for a loan. "I was reluctant. I had made him loans before and sometimes you don't get them back when you lend to relatives." He admitted he phoned Schultz in Vancouver and got the loan from a man he had known only a short time. The jurors' faces showed they found this odd.

At the end of his ten-hour performance, Sommers was like a balloon with a slow leak. His confidence was gone, his voice at times was almost inaudible, and his chiselled features seemed to sag. Sommers knew better than anyone that his vague responses left more questions unanswered than answered, and the jury probably was filling in the blanks for themselves. His story didn't challenge the detailed accusations of Eversfield and some of the others, and while the documentation they presented was less than complete, it hurt him.

When Sommers left the box, Nicholson said he would not call Wick Gray to testify. The lawyer said his client's defence would have taken two weeks to present and was not necessary because it was covered in evidence already introduced at the trial. This was hardly convincing but may have been Nicholson's best move in a no-win situation. The clearly distraught Gray was not up to facing days of testimony, and he might have blurted out anything under the heat of cross-examination. From the outset, he was the accused suffering the most from stress.

The trial had dragged on since May 1 through one of Vancouver's loveliest and warmest summers in years, interrupted several times by illnesses and punctuated by long, tedious, legal arguments. The jurors were flagging. They asked Judge Wilson if they might have a short holiday to spend time with their children and families. When the trial was adjourned until August 25, they welcomed the judge's announcement like kids let out of school. With the bulk of the evidence heard, only the last shots remained to be fired. It had been a lengthy, confusing, tiring battle. Judge Wilson told the jurors, "I hope you get some benefit from your holiday. Come back strong; you will have to listen to a great deal of argument when you return."

For the lawyers it was time to prepare their final summations. For Sommers, Schultz, and the Grays, it was another delay as they awaited the jury's decision. They already had brief experience of life behind bars; conviction could mean long jail sentences.

The Defence Rests

When Judge Wilson called the summer recess on Day 58 of the trial, the jury had high hopes of hearing final testimony by early September. The twelve of them came back from their holiday in the last week of August, sure that their task was almost done. It was not.

Charles Eversfield was the principal target of defence lawyers as they summed up their cases. They went after him from every angle, hoping to convince the jury he was a complete liar who hadn't uttered an honest word. His character was assailed; Alfred Bull, representing Schultz, didn't even like his eyes. The lawyer contended that Eversfield couldn't face his questioners squarely. "He has eyes," Bull told the jury. "So has a snake." Bull accused Eversfield of being "a thief, a forger, a blackmailer, and an accomplice if there was a crime." He suggested the case was "instigated to destroy the Social Credit party." Bull tied Eversfield to Gibson, Sturdy, and the *Vancouver Sun*, all participants in the plot. His efforts to conjure up a national political conspiracy increasingly sounded like far-fetched theatrics. The jury was unimpressed.

Walter Owen, counsel for BCFP, blasted the Crown for "doing everything possible" to prevent the case from coming to trial and failing in its responsibility to the people of the province. He said the tardiness had deprived the company of the evidence of Munro. The late president was a man who knew all about the various transactions and would have been a sound material witness, said Owen. He contended Daniels had tried to "poison the public mind against Munro," and with the president gone he could say whatever he wanted.

J.R. Nicholson said Wick Gray had not testified because he was loyal to people who gave money to the Socreds and was honour bound to keep information about donations secret. It would be distasteful and embarrassing to do otherwise, argued the lawyer, who added that any money Gray handled had been either personal loans to Sommers or funds intended for Social Credit Party coffers. He was not, as the Crown had contended, the middleman in a conspiracy, passing money received from Schultz and BCFP to the minister. The increasingly nervous Gray fidgeted, looking as though embarrassment was much farther from his mind than the spectre of jail.

On September 2 the hopes of an early end to the trial died. The court was told a woman juror was suffering from jaundice and would need to be away for four to six weeks. Two doctors were called, who confirmed her illness.

The weary judge told the court that it was permissible for the trial to continue one juror short. This was agreeable to him and the prosecution, but not to the defence, which wanted all twelve available to vote on the verdict. Once again the trial was adjourned. Jurors would not return until October 20.

On resumption of the case after the six-week break, Angelo Branca spoke for six hours, summing up Sommers' defence. The veteran lawyer asked the jury to give his client the benefit of the doubt in this complicated case with its confusing and contradictory evidence. He tried to explain away Sommers' damaging memory losses, which more than anything else had made him appear guilty. Many witnesses could not remember details from years back, said Branca. It was "only Eversfield who could reach up, recreate and relive conversations dealing with every instance that occurred starting back in 1953." Referring to the repayment of Sommers' loans from the bank by an unknown party, Branca pleaded with the jury "not to hold that against us." He stressed it was not an offence to accept loans, gifts, or payments for expenses, but only wrong if they influenced a decision. Branca argued the evidence against Sommers did not support this. The lawyer contended Eversfield had an ulterior motive and urged jurors to give its "stamp of approval to a man in public office who has done much for the province of B.C." Branca said Judge Wilson might find Eversfield was an accomplice and he warned of the danger of accepting uncorroborated evidence from such a person. However, Eversfield was well represented by David Sturdy from the beginning, and as a prosecution witness was unlikely to be charged.

Prosecutor Dryer took five days for his summation, reading long, long passages from the transcript, going back over dates, details, and the complexities of the various transactions. The prosecutor contended that all defence claims were inconsistent with the documentation presented. For example, he attacked BCFP's claim that money passed to Schultz was for consulting work. Holding up some of the relevant documents tabled during Daniels' testimony, which described work done for BCFP by C.D. Schultz and Associates, Dryer asked, "Would any man in his right mind, let alone the hard-headed businessmen of BCFP, pay $15,000 for these?" The prosecutor derided Schultz's evidence, declaring that no one with any sense would hire the inexperienced Wick Gray to do public relations work.

The press dubbed the performance a "talkathon." At times the jury seemed lost in the welter of references and cross-references, visibly tiring of the whole affair. It had been a long time since May, when they were selected from more than 100 people for the job that was not yet completed. They must have asked themselves more than once, "Why me?"

Following Dryer's statement, Judge Wilson told the jury he was taking a new step in Canadian judicial procedure and would break his summation into three parts. It would first cover the conspiracy charge involving all of the accused; then the twelve charges against the Grays, Schultz, BCFP, and other companies for offering bribes; and finally the seven charges against Sommers for accepting them. All other counts had been dismissed at various times. The defence objected to this proposition, but the judge was not swayed from his decision.

Wilson began his summation of the conspiracy charge on October 28 and ordered the jury to be confined for the first time since the trial began. They were housed in the Devonshire Hotel across the street from the courthouse.

The jurors were housed in the Devonshire Hotel, just west of the Georgia Hotel in this mid-1950s shot of the intersection of Georgia and Granville streets in Vancouver, the hub of the city. The jurors crossed Georgia Street from the hotel to the courthouse as they weighed the fate of the four accused.

The judge told the jurors he would be reading his charge—"an unfortunate way to do things but the complications of this case are such that I cannot trust myself or my memory and must read." He said months of evidence had gone through the wringer and he wanted the jurors to wipe their minds clear of all that they had read and heard of the case outside the courtroom. They must deal strictly with what they had heard during the court proceedings. It would be no easy task. Political rhetoric about Sommers, as well as reports of various bribery and corruption hearings, had dominated the news for a long time.

Judge Wilson told the jury that he found Eversfield was a co-conspirator in the affair, and he repeated the warning about accepting uncorroborated evidence from such a witness. He also stated that the only direct evidence against BCFP came from a former employee, Trevor Daniels, and it had been alleged that he was a man with a grudge against the company and its chief officer, the late Hector Munro. The judge appeared to suggest that jurors should not believe everything they had heard from these two men in particular, but it was difficult to understand what part of the testimony the jurors were supposed to ignore.

In his fourteen-hour charge, Judge Wilson said he found the financial transactions and the transfer of money to Sommers unusual, curious, and devious. He emphasized that there was no documentation to back up the claims that they were loans. He said the fact that money was sent in cash, by wire, and as bonds was a "strong feature in the Crown case," as was the fact that the loans to Sommers were not paid by cheque. He added, "I remind you that a loan made for a corrupt purpose is just as criminal as a gift for a corrupt purpose." Judge Wilson cited as significant the removal of files from Schultz's office to an employee's home as soon as the Lord Commission was ordered. He dismissed Alfred Bull's contention that there was a Liberal plot to destroy the Social Credit government as a "red herring."

Judge Wilson ended his first charge to the jury at 3:07 p.m. on Thursday, October 30. He had dealt with more than two million words of testimony and 1,060 exhibits presented over 73 sitting days. The jury was then sent from the courtroom as the judge listened to the arguments of defence lawyers for two hours as they requested changes in his charge. Wilson recalled the twelve and dealt with 22 minor points.

Sommers and his co-accused had been permitted to sit at a table with their lawyers during much of the trial. Now they were back in the prisoners' box. As Judge Wilson spoke, Sommers read a large legal tome, Schultz at times dozed, and John Gray stared at the jurors. The increasingly agitated Wick Gray nibbled on a finger and twitched nervously, unable to sit still.

After only two hours of deliberation, at about 9 p.m., the jury foreman told Judge Wilson that he felt it would take the better part of the next day at least before they would reach a decision on the conspiracy count. "That is very commendable," said Judge Wilson, "God speed you in your work and good night." Clutching their voluminous folders jammed with documents, the jurors rushed across rainswept Georgia Street to the Devonshire Hotel. The accused remained free on bail. It was to be an agonizing wait of more than 48 hours before they heard the verdict on the first of the three sections of charges against them.

Final Curtain

Just after 4 p.m. Saturday afternoon, the jury told Sheriff Edwin Wells that it had a verdict. Chief Justice Wilson announced that the court would reconvene at 7.30 p.m. News travelled quickly, and crowds gathered outside in the rain for the final act, a time of tragedy or triumph for the accused. David Sturdy was among those who filed in just after 7 p.m. Bennett was on holiday in Phoenix, Arizona, far from questioning reporters who would ask about his government's handling of the affair and Bonner's role, especially if the jury returned a guilty verdict.

Charlie Schultz was the first of the accused to arrive at the courthouse. He told reporters he had spent the day painting. The Gray brothers came together. It was their second trip that day because a cruel crank phone call had brought them to the courthouse earlier in the afternoon. John Gray commented, "I am confident, I really am." Younger brother Wick, whose sixth child had been born during the trial, looked wretched.

Sommers, trademark cigarette holder clamped between his teeth, maintained his debonair pose when he arrived just before 7.30 p.m. He told those who inquired that he had been napping at Deep Cove, a North Vancouver suburb where he had been staying. Asked how he felt, Sommers replied, "Oh, as usual, but that covers a multitude." Reporters asked what significance he placed on the length of the jury deliberation, which was longer than anyone expected. Sommers answered, "You people have more experience at these things than I have." When it was mentioned that he didn't seem concerned or worried, he replied, "I take it as it comes."

As the jurors filed in they took the same chairs they had occupied for months, looking everywhere around the tense, packed room except at the four accused in the prisoners' box. They had dined together at the Devonshire for what they hoped was close to the last time. Having cleared their first major hurdle, the male members had presented the three women jurors with corsages, which they wore into court, the pink flowers looking very much out of place. This was no celebration. The strain showed in the faces of the women, who were pale and drawn.

Judge Wilson entered quickly, and court clerk Jacob Abrahams immediately asked the jury, "Have you reached your verdict?" Less than a minute after the start of proceedings, foreman Eric Miller was on his feet. In a halting voice he said there were verdicts on the conspiracy counts. Miller was nervous, caught up in the drama of the moment. Sommers' name was called first and he stood. His world came crashing down as Miller said, "Guilty." Sommers' body jerked and he chewed on his lower lip, but otherwise his expression didn't change, his composure barely altered. Under the law, as a convicted felon, he immediately lost his seat in the legislature.

Wick Gray was a worried, pathetic figure. His pink woollen sweater looked incongruous beside the dark suits of his colleagues. It was his turn to rise and he slowly got to his feet. When Miller intoned "Guilty," Gray bent forward and clasped his hands over his eyes. He looked as though he might fall, but he didn't. The jury also found Gray's two companies guilty in the plot. Wick's brother John gasped with relief when the foreman said, "There is disagreement as to his innocence or guilt," and he immediately put his arm around his anguished brother. Charlie Schultz had cause to smile with relief when Miller stated there was also disagreement in his case. BCFP was found not guilty. In the public gallery, Wally McCutcheon smiled broadly. The jury had found the tea party and the subsequent meeting in Victoria apparently as innocent as the one attended by Alice in Wonderland.

The BCFP verdict was particularly confusing for anyone who had heard or read the evidence of the company's former chief financial officer, Trevor Daniels. How could BCFP be "not guilty" if both Wick Gray and Sommers were guilty? Why had the jury been undecided about Schultz when so much emanated from his office? Even though Judge Wilson had cautioned that Daniels might hold a grudge, how could the jury decide BCFP was innocent when it seemed to be the biggest beneficiary?

The packed galleries buzzed with the findings as spectators leaned forward for a better look at the accused. Sheriff Wells called for order and the noise subsided. Sommers and Wick Gray were remanded in custody for sentence while John Gray and Charlie Schultz remained free on bail. No one knew if there would be new trials because of the jury's inability to reach a unanimous decision, and the bribery charges still remained to be dealt with.

Sommers and Gray were taken down a flight of white stairs from the courtroom to the cells. Sommers spoke briefly with his lawyer before being led away. John Gray hugged and comforted his brother before Wick was escorted out, still in a daze. For Sommers and Gray there was the possibility of an appeal, but Sommers' political career was over, crashing to an abrupt end as quickly as it had soared in triumph only a few years earlier.

There was another humiliation for Sommers before the night was over. A crowd waited outside in the rain to ogle the ex-minister as he and Gray were handcuffed and escorted from the courthouse to the local jail for the weekend. Within a few hours a doctor was called to examine Gray, who was near collapse.

The case established some firsts in B.C. legal history. The media claimed it was the longest trial in the province to that date, and the 52.5 hours of jury deliberation was also claimed as a record. The *Province* newspaper maintained that it was the first time in the British Commonwealth that a cabinet minister had been convicted of conspiracy to accept bribes.

The guilty verdicts brought immediate cries from political opponents, the media, and the public. There were demands for everything from Bonner's head on a plate to a general election. The attorney general's handling of the affair was bitterly attacked, with accusations of cover-up and protection of friends of the government. There were demands for a total overhaul of the system of granting FMLs. Many were upset that BCFP got off scot-free.

The *Sun* was first off the mark with a blistering front-page editorial that blamed Bonner for just about everything but the great Vancouver fire of 1886. "Resign, Mr. Bonner," said the headline. The *Sun* charged the attorney general with "scandalously delaying the process of justice in the bribery-conspiracy case involving one of his cabinet associates."

In fairness, they gave the former infantryman space the next day for a battling response. "Resign? Hell, no," fired back the angry Bonner in a long written statement. He said he still was not in a legal position to comment on the case itself, but he blasted the *Sun*, maintaining the government was not going to be dictated to by newspaper barons. His best shot was an observation that Vancouver had two major problems—polluted beaches and "Don Cromie's management of the *Vancouver Sun*. Both are a distinct disadvantage to the community. Mr. Cromie is using the paper as a rich man's toy," he wrote. The war of words raged on as Bonner faced a great army of critics.

While the combatants slugged away, the trial went on. Monday found Sommers and Gray back in court with the other two accused to face the remaining nineteen charges, twelve that they and their companies gave bribes and seven that Sommers received them.

When he began the second charge, Judge Wilson told the jurors, "I am keenly aware of the fact that my voice must be beginning to sound to you like a dentist's drill." He added there was nothing he could do about it. "I have to deal as faithfully as ever with the part of the trial that remains to be disposed of."

It didn't take too long. He reviewed the evidence, and two days later the jury came back with its second set of decisions. Sommers was found guilty on five counts of accepting bribes, with disagreement on two others; Wick Gray was convicted on eight counts of giving bribes, with disagreement on two; Schultz was not guilty on four, with disagreement on five; John Gray was not guilty on two, with disagreement on two others. Wick Gray's companies, PCS and Evergreen, were found guilty on some counts with disagreement on others; Charlie Schultz's company and BCFP were found not guilty on some counts with disagreement on others. The public was confused again by the decisions. Sommers and Wick Gray were nailed hard while everyone else escaped. If Sommers accepted bribes and Gray paid them, where did the money come from?

Prosecutor Dryer told reporters that it was up to Bonner to decide if there should be a new trial on the charges where the jury disagreed. Veteran lawyers commented that in cases like this it was common for the Crown to order a "stay of proceedings" and take no further action. This was the course Bonner followed, and there were many who disagreed with his decision.

The media continued to call for Bonner's head, particularly the *Sun*, and there were reports of widespread unhappiness in Socred ranks. A poll of backbenchers showed that none thought the attorney general should resign, but support was lukewarm.

Bonner had a brief moment of revenge on November 7 when Judge Wilson fined the *Sun* for contempt. The defence had objected to a headline that it claimed was slanted and highly prejudicial. It had called Wick Gray a "Kingpin" in the affair. Wilson praised the reporting during the case but said this headline was "regrettable." He fined the *Sun* and publisher Don Cromie $5,000. In Victoria, Bonner wryly observed, "Sometimes we do get good news."

Prosecutor Vic Dryer said he had lost fifteen pounds during the trial, and his assistant Stu McMorran also admitted to losing weight under the pressure. Jury foreman Eric Miller allowed, "It was a terrific

Don Cromie ran the Sun *newspaper started by his father until the early 1960s. He loved big headlines and flashy front pages, though sometimes they got him in trouble.*

emotional strain. I'm completely exhausted." Lawyer Alfred Bull told reporters, "Am I glad it's over? Now what do you think?" Some jurors, who had received six dollars for each sitting, said they had lost money. One maintained that being away from his job had cost him close to $2,000.

Charlie Schultz exhibited some of the bounce-back optimism of the *Peanuts* cartoon's Charlie Brown, written and created by another Charles Schultz. He did not seem too concerned about the verdicts one way or the other, nor did he express any interest in knowing whether the Crown might lay new charges. When asked how he felt, Schultz replied it didn't matter, "I'm ruined anyway." He said his former empire was down to a two-room holdout on three empty floors of an office building. With a grin he maintained, "It's still the best firm in Canada." The once powerful, booming business had been ruined by political scandal and the indecisive verdict that left his reputation in tatters.

While Sommers and Gray were transported back to Oakalla Prison Farm to await sentencing, there were sighs of relief from most other players in the drama. Even Judge Wilson, who was on the eve of his sixtieth birthday, agreed to pose for a picture as he smoked his favourite pipe. He admitted, "[I am] very tired and I hope I can do some plain loafing for a while." He voiced an ambition to travel in Europe.

The trial was over, but not the ramifications of the case, and sentencing was still to come. There was one more headline-grabbing twist when a caller to the courthouse claimed he had overheard a plot to "get" Judge Wilson. While there were few details and it sounded far-fetched, the report was not ignored and it resulted in tighter security for the judge during the remainder of the proceedings. There were no further incidents.

Some of the players gained relief, but this was a bleak time for Sommers and Gray. They faced what could be long years in jail, and Judge Wilson was known for pronouncing heavy sentences. November 14 was set as the day of decision.

November 14

Judge Wilson looked grim as he took his seat and stared directly at Sommers and Wick Gray. Both men were tense, but Gray did not look as distraught as he had on his last appearance in the dock.

Wilson did not mince words. "I do not like hitting men when they are down as both of you are, but this is an exceptional case and requires comment. There is evidence both of you have befouled the political and moral atmosphere of this province for a period of many years, resorting to every sort of shape and device to conceal your iniquities." The judge's words made clear what was coming. This was not to be a slap on the wrist. There would be no suspended sentence; both the accused were facing jail terms.

Looking intently at Sommers, Judge Wilson said he hoped the former minister had not done much damage to the traditional respect for government through his conduct. He said he disagreed with the contention of defence lawyers that a sentence on the conspiracy charge, on which each had been convicted, should "swallow up the others." The jury had also found Sommers guilty of five bribery counts and Gray of eight.

Judge Wilson doled out his ruling. He decided there would be five counts against each man, each of these to carry a one-year sentence. Other counts would run concurrently, meaning they would be "swallowed up" by the first five. With a year on each charge, this amounted to five years in jail for Sommers. As he grasped the full meaning, he swayed and stared dully at the rail of the prisoners' box. All eyes in the courtroom were then trained on Wick Gray. How would he react? He too received a total of five years but, surprisingly, showed little emotion. Judge Wilson also fined Gray's companies $30,000.

There were whispers among the lawyers and the public about the severity of the sentences. No doubt there would be an appeal. There had obviously been considerable disagreement among the jurors, as they had taken an unprecedented total of 75 hours to reach all their verdicts.

Sommers and Gray were led away once more down the white stairs to the cells. Again a curious crowd waited outside to watch Sommers, the fallen star. Some revelled in witnessing the fall of the mighty. Unlike Judge Wilson, they didn't mind in the least hitting a man when he was down.

Bonner issued an official statement, maintaining the government had acted "firmly and conscientiously" in handling the case, still adamant that Sturdy had no real evidence when they first met. He said, "It was not until November 1957 that lawyers decided there was enough evidence to prosecute Sommers."

Only hours after the statement was released, Bonner talked to reporters from the *Province* and the *Sun* about his own feelings. He said that when he first heard that something was wrong, "my reaction was one of complete disbelief. I knew Mr. Sommers and never had any reason to doubt his application to his work. I had an admiration for his apparent ability at that time." Bonner continued, "Now that the trial is over, I am not, like some others, going to heap recrimination on him. He has been dealt with by due process of the law. It was a painful obligation for me to carry out." Bonner later repeated he always had the gravest doubts that the Crown's case would produce a conviction, adding, "If Sommers hadn't taken the stand in his own defence, I don't think he would have been [convicted]."

When he was asked about David Sturdy by the *Province*'s Gordon McCallum, Bonner commented, "I still think that when Sturdy came to see me on December 7, 1955, the only purpose was to involve this office in some way. He never did come back."

Summing up, as lawyers are wont to do, the attorney general covered fourteen months of police investigation with the comment, "There is in fact, to this day, no evidence that any timber company has improperly obtained a forest management licence." He added that the department was proven clean of any improprieties in an examination undertaken by Ray Williston when he took over the forest portfolio.

The government wasted no time in calling a by-election to replace Sommers. Bonner, in Bennett's absence, announced it would be held December 15. A crowd of 200 enthusiastically nominated Donald Brothers, a 36-year-old Trail lawyer. He promised more jobs and economic improvements. Sommers' name wasn't even mentioned. Despite the scandals and convictions, Brothers held the seat for the Socreds as, once again, the vote was split. He was a winner with only 30.1 percent of the popular vote. Following the win, Sommers made

Donald Brothers, a 36-year-old Trail lawyer, represented Social Credit in the by-election following Sommers' conviction. At his nomination meeting, Sommers' name was not even mentioned. The by-election was a tough four-way fight, and Brothers won by a whisker with only 30.1 percent of the popular vote and 3,170 votes. The CCF took 26.63 percent of the vote; the Liberals, 22.43 percent; the Tories, 20.87 percent.

the cryptic comment that the result "vindicates father," which most took to be a reference to Bennett.

In the midst of the by-election, the attorney general's department proposed to appeal Judge Wilson's sentencing decision and request longer jail terms. An enraged Sommers, who was out on bail, phoned Bonner to protest the move, and it did fail to come about. In the interim, Sommers' anger worried the Socreds, who feared he might hit back during the by-election with derogatory comments about government activities. He didn't.

Lawyer Angelo Branca filed Sommers' appeal in the B.C. Supreme Court, as did J.R. Nicholson for Gray. Until February 16, the day set for the hearing, Sommers was free on $34,000 bail; $24,000 put up by Fraser Valley Socred MLA Irvine Corbett and $10,000 provided by Sommers' son-in-law John Abrosino, of California. Gray was out on $30,000 bail.

Branca said he would argue the point already ruled on by Judge Wilson that the charges should not have been put to the jury because they were laid long after the time limit permitted by law. This was the old law/new law argument that the judge had himself brought to the attention of all the other lawyers in the court.

Nicholson also maintained that the charges were not properly served, that testimony was heard on 39 charges, some of which were later thrown out, and that the "Kingpin" headline and article, for which the *Sun* was fined for contempt of court, was prejudicial. Nicholson also repeated his contention that a minister was not an official under the law as then written and therefore could not be charged, which prosecutor Dryer labelled an "astounding" proposal. Nicholson admitted that Judge Wilson had thrown out this argument at the trial, but argued that the ruling was wrong. The appeal hearing lasted four days.

On March 19 the court dismissed the appeals by a two-to-one vote. Justices H.I. Bird and F.A. Shepherd voted against and Justice H.W. Davey for the defence. The latter accepted Nicholson's argument about Sommers not being an official and also agreed the prosecution was too late.

Sommers and Gray were re-arrested and sent back to jail. Their lawyers appealed the verdict to the Supreme Court of Canada. In Victoria, Mrs. Sommers told reporters, "I will wait forever if necessary. Bob has been a wonderful husband and father to our children. I don't care what anybody says, he is a good man." Mrs. Sommers indicated she would go back to work to support the family. She added that she was fed up with politics and said, "I didn't want him to go into them in the first place."

Backbencher Cyril Shelford, a gangly rancher from the north who gained a reputation as one of the most honest politicians of the period, was deeply concerned about the effect the whole affair had on Sommers' wife and school-aged children, who were "called all sorts of names by the other kids." Perfect strangers phoned the family home and told Mrs. Sommers to keep "her dirty, crooked kids out of school" so they wouldn't lead others astray.

Irvine Corbett and Shelford attended many of the trial sessions. Shelford commented afterward that they had expected fireworks, particularly from Sommers' attorney, Angelo Branca, but said, "I was never so disappointed in my life. Branca and the other lawyers argued for hours about what seemed to be very minor points, like whether Sommers was an official or not. This made little sense to me. It seemed that the real question should be: How can Sommers be guilty of taking a bribe if no company gave him any money?"

After the verdicts came down, the Sommers' case continued to haunt the legislature. Shelford, who had earlier made his unhappiness at the handling of the whole case public, criticized Bonner, stressing he had been very disturbed for a long time. In his book *From Snowshoes to Politics,* Shelford wrote, "I asked many times that the case be brought to trial quickly rather than letting it drag on for months."

On March 23 the B.C. Supreme Court adjourned an appeal launched by the defence against the length of Judge Wilson's sentences, pending the outcome of the appeal of the verdict at the Supreme Court of Canada. Supreme Court officials said it was customary for an appeal on behalf of persons being held in jail to get a priority hearing, so on April 13 a date of April 28 was set for the appeal. For two days Branca and Nicholson made their case. The court reserved judgment, stating that a decision would be announced as soon as possible. For Sommers and Gray, this was their last chance to avoid a lengthy term in jail.

Seven weeks later, on June 25, the justices unanimously dismissed their appeals. Mr. Justice Gerald Fauteux wrote, "I am unable to agree with the proposition that the [criminal] code applies only to non-political officials as distinguished from political officials." He also noted that in common law, the "corruption of any official, either judicial or ministerial, is an offence and the distinction between political and non-political is of no significance."

The Supreme Court agreed with the earlier B.C. Appeal Court majority decision. The highest court in the land ruled that because the old code, which stipulated a charge must be laid within two years, had been repealed before the two years had expired in this case, the time limit did not apply. The court also stated that while the offences were committed before the new code came into effect in 1955, they must be tried under the new code. Observers noted that Judge Wilson had made a similar ruling and praised him, pointing out that his handling of the long, complicated case did not produce a successful appeal, and none of his rulings during the trial were overturned.

At the end of June the public learned from the media that Sommers was in Oakalla jail hospital, under observation for a minor heart problem. Officials said hospitalization meant he didn't have the daily climb of many flights of stairs inside the prison.

As Sommers rested, the B.C. Court of Appeal dealt with the one remaining decision still undecided, the length of the sentences. The old code/new code argument and decision affected the terms. The court ruled that instead of one-year consecutive sentences on the conspiracy and bribery charges against the pair amounting to five years, it would be five years on the conspiracy charge and one-year for all of the bribery counts, to run concurrently. Gray had three more bribery convictions than Sommers, but it would not mean he would spend any more time in jail.

The news was relayed to Sommers at Vancouver General Hospital, where he had been transferred for treatment of his heart problem. He was "shattered" by the news, the papers reported. The prison doctor at Oakalla was tagged to deliver the news to Gray in case the already overwrought man collapsed. He didn't, although it was stated he was surprised and distressed. Gray was in the penitentiary only a little more than a week when the *Sun* reported that his family had started to ask about early parole. Parole officers said it was highly unlikely there would be parole for Gray or Sommers until they had served at least half their sentences.

Gray was given some special consideration because of his mental state. He was not put in the segregation area, which was routine for the first thirty days for most prisoners. Claustrophobia was among his problems, and he was kept in an area where he was not isolated and was free to walk the corridors. Warden Fred Cummins said he permitted this after interviewing Gray, as he did all new prisoners. The warden stated that it wasn't part of his job to produce mental breakdowns.

After serving two years and four months, Sommers and Gray were paroled. Little is known of Gray's experiences behind bars, but Sommers used his time there to his own advantage, taking correspondence courses from Queens University and learning much about a musical instrument he'd never played before, the piano.

LOOKING BACK

The judge and jury worked hard to reach the conclusions that sent only two men to prison and let the others off, although with their lives much altered. The comments of participants looking back at events shed some light on the ins and outs of the Sommers affair.

Old Scars

It was four years after being defeated by his archenemy, "the socialist hordes," that the old warrior W.A.C. Bennett brought himself to confess what had been his worst experience in twenty years as premier. In retirement at his Kelowna home in 1976, a reporter asked Bennett if the loss to the NDP had been his biggest blow. Without hesitation he said no, it was the Sommers affair.

Bennett finally revealed that when the bribery rumours were brought to his attention, he had hired the best private detective in Vancouver to probe the charges. "He came back and said there was nothing to it, nothing but straight politics. That is the reason I didn't think there was anything to it," said Bennett. He still didn't think "there was much to it."

By 1976 the battle was long over, but Bennett still wouldn't admit defeat. "I think it was stupid. He was an honourable man, he was my best debater. His daughter was getting married and he needed some carpets or something," said the ex-premier, either having forgotten the details of his lowest point or still wanting to fudge the issue as he had twenty years earlier. Bennett said Sommers' friends had helped him out. "I think he intended to pay them in the end and I am sure he did," he added.

Bennett said that after the affair began he had forestry department personnel and other public servants search documents and records "to see if Sommers had given one single red cent of concessions to anybody in that department and they couldn't find anything." Looking back, he assessed Sommers' actions by saying "bad judgment, bad judgment." W.A.C. would neither confirm nor deny that during her husband's incarceration he provided Nona Sommers with a monthly stipend delivered through a family member in Victoria.

Bennett's comments brought out other veterans of the great scandal to refight old issues. Within days of the ex-premier's reminiscing, J.O. Wilson, the man who presided at Sommers' trial and jailed him, struck back in a letter to the editor of the *Sun*. The retired chief justice stated the affair was long past and he would have preferred "to leave the corpse of the Sommers case buried," but he had to challenge Bennett's comments. He saw them as criticism of his handling of the case and of the jury's verdict. Wilson wrote that the Sommers case had much substance to it, rather than nothing, as Bennett contended.

Wilson questioned why Bennett had gone to a private detective to probe the rumours. "Why not the police forces of the province?" He said Sommers was convicted of one charge of conspiracy and five of bribery, verdicts upheld by the appeal court. "Would any fair minded person say there was nothing to it?" Wilson asked, arguing that the minister's actions at the time were hardly those of an honourable man. He agreed with Bennett that Sommers had been stupid, "but so is the conduct of most criminals." The man who was on the bench, and who heard it all, said Sommers was defended by "some of the ablest criminal counsel in B.C."

Wilson acknowledged that Sommers had paid his debt to society and wished him well, hoping that "he is now, as Bennett says, an honourable man." Wilson said his letter was not written to hurt Sommers, but to correct some inaccuracies that perhaps "reflect on the judgment of the jury which tried this memorable case."

This exchange brought Sommers into action from his home on Vancouver Island. He wrote that the only FML in question was #22, the one given to BCFP, and the company had been acquitted of the conspiracy charge. He said Wilson had detailed the five bribery charges, and he felt "any fair minded and courageous ex-judge" would have been equally precise in naming the FML applicants who paid the amounts cited and "who in turn received favours from me." Sommers challenged Wilson to amend his letter and include the exact names. He stated that if Wilson did not, "his silence will speak volumes to all those who stood by me and who might have been interested in the past judicial exercise known as the Sommers case." Wilson did not respond to Sommers' challenge

Following the appearance of the former minister's letter, several reporters contacted Sommers. He commented that he "always had the highest regard for W.A.C. Bennett." Asked if he had known that Bennett had a private detective investigate the allegations against him, Sommers replied, "I don't care who investigated who. I know what I did."

On the same page as Sommers' letter was one from Tom Norris, a prominent lawyer who participated in some of B.C.'s most famous cases before being made a judge. Norris, who had no part in the Sommers case but who could never ignore a scrap, stated that he thought Wilson's response to Bennett, whom Norris never liked, was a "perfectly splendid letter and quite proper for the occasion." A few other retired warriors threw in their comments, while others shared the view that the corpse of the Sommers affair was better left buried. The 1976 mini-replay of Bennett's lowest point in a tumultuous, twenty-year record run as B.C.'s premier went quietly into history.

The past was overhauled again in some taped conversations between two old curmudgeons, leading players in the crisis. Years after he retired as deputy minister of forests, Dr. C.D. Orchard put together an oral history of his years in forestry and discussed the Sommers case with the retired Gordon Gibson. The crusty Dr. Orchard's dislike of his former minister hadn't diminished with the years, and he described him as "the acquisitive Mr. Sommers." He stressed that department officials had not been involved in any improprieties, and Gibson agreed. Dr. Orchard said that after he left the government he was told by various sources that any FML aspirant who applied during 1954 and 1955 knew exactly what it would cost to have an application considered. Gibson suggested payments could have been as high as $200,000, contending that it was a three-way split between Schultz, Gray, and Sommers. A characteristic of the reminiscences of elderly gentlemen, however, is a tendency to exaggeration and one-upmanship.

The authors of *Forests, Power and Policy,* a biography of Ray Williston published in 1997, describe how, immediately upon succeeding Sommers as minister of forests, Williston ordered a full-scale investigation of the department. He was looking for corruption because the media was hammering on the point that the bribery scandal went far beyond Sommers. Williston's biographers write, "Ray's investigations, however, proved to his satisfaction that 'there was not one single thing out of place when we opened up the books.' Since all forest companies had to apply in the same way for FMLs and all went through the same processing steps, the only point at which any fixing could have been done was when the minister chose to consider or not consider an application for recommendation to cabinet."

The book records Williston's view that "to this day, I'm sure that if Charlie Schultz acted as representative for a company applying for an FML, that company received consideration. And if certain other agents presented an application, it never got to the stage where it received consideration. I'm as sure to this day as I was then that Sommers alone juggled the books; some applications received immediate consideration, others never got looked at."

Proud of his accomplishments during his years as minister, Williston offered to resign if anyone could find 50 cents out of place.

Vancouver Sun columnist Barry Mather joked, "It's only a few years since we'd be asked to find a nickel out of place, but Williston is asking us to find fifty cents!"

The passage of time has tempered the views of another old warrior of B.C.'s fiercest political battle. Deane Finlayson, whose political career died at the hands of Bennett and the Socreds, was a key figure in the Sommers case. Since 1961, when Sommers was released from jail, he and Finlayson have lived only about twenty miles from each other on Vancouver Island, although they haven't met in all that time.

Compared to his fierce denunciations of 45 years earlier, Finlayson in 1999 took a different view, seeing Sommers as a victim and wondering how his offences would be viewed today in a world of changing morality. "He was a really nice guy who suffered from his lack of knowledge and experience in politics. He was thrown in with people who wanted something and took advantage of him," Finlayson said. As Tory leader for about six years in the 1950s, Finlayson ran twice for a seat in the legislature but was defeated. His second attempt was in the hotly contested 1956 election, when Sommers' libel action kept information about the allegations against him from the public. "I couldn't be silenced," said Finlayson, who ignored the threat of a contempt charge from Sommers' lawyer and, in a gutsy speech in North Vancouver, tried to bring home to the people of B.C. the importance of the allegations against the minister. Finlayson's hopes of election soared following the speech, but he was crushed by the Socred machine and all its promises when the voting actually took place.

Finlayson, a silver-haired, erect, 80-year-old, said he had no regrets about his aborted political career. Asked what got him into politics, he smilingly pointed a finger at his temple and twisted it. When that career ended, he returned to his real estate business in Nanaimo, where he is still active as a Board of Trade member. Finlayson said that when John Diefenbaker was in power in Ottawa, he was offered a good position in the public service, but he rejected it because it would require him to live in Ottawa, and his heart would always be on the West Coast with the sea, the forests, and the islands of B.C.

Finlayson said the Conservative Party was now dead provincially in B.C., with no signs of a rebirth, although he saw slight stirrings at the federal level. In the spring of 1999 he despaired of the performance of Premier Glen Clark and his NDP government, fearing that a total collapse of the provincial economy was not out of the question. The

Deane Finlayson revisited his political past in 1999, expressing sympathy for Sommers. Finlayson said he had no regrets about his own aborted political career. He never forgot the unforgiving nature of his former profession, and his final comment on the old political war was, "For Sommers, it was simply the brutality of politics."

forest industry was in dire straits, said Finlayson, and nobody seemed to have any idea how to fix it, with little agreement between government, industry, the unions, Native peoples, or the environmental movement.

Finlayson said he was concerned about the lowering of moral and ethical standards within communities and governments. He would have preferred to see government set the standard rather than manipulate it using all the tricks available. "It is time for people to recognize the advantages they have in this province and in this country and to get together to do something to keep us strong and secure," opined the old politician.

As one of its victims, he had never forgotten the unforgiving nature of his former profession and had a final comment on the toll of the old political war—"For Sommers, it was simply the brutality of politics."

In his autobiography, respected Socred MLA Cyril Shelford states, "Even when Bob Sommers went to jail, the debate in the legislature continued. Many of us in the backbench were left disillusioned by the lack of straightforward information we received on the government's strategy in handling the case. The only apparent reason for the long delay in bringing the case before the courts was to keep it in limbo until after the 1956 election. Many of us disagreed strongly with this strategy. My position was very clear from the start. When serious charges are made against a minister of the government, he should be asked to step aside until he is either cleared or convicted." Shelford maintained this should be done as quickly as possible for the good of the minister involved, to protect the good name of the party, and more important still, to re-establish the trust people once placed in government. Shelford cited instances in the U.K. of ministers resigning or being pushed out immediately after charges were made against them and of quick investigations of the allegations. He felt a similar process should apply in B.C.

Shelford, ever a supporter of a better democratic process, also commented, "Today it's nearly unheard of for government members to vote against the government, no matter what they do. There's no doubt that the day of the independent thinker in politics has gone. I think this is a tremendous loss to the democratic system." He said it stifles new ideas and creative solutions. Cyril Shelford continues to work behind the scenes to try to improve the kind of democracy practised in B.C.

"All For the People"

When he was interviewed nearly a half century after the allegations from Gordon Gibson, Bob Sommers still maintained that all he ever got from BCFP was $750,000 for the people of British Columbia. It was part of the price exacted from E.P. Taylor for FML #22 and was approximately the cost of building a logging road that would help to open up the west coast of Vancouver Island to the public. "That was all there was to it," said the former forests minister, contending that he was innocent of the crimes that sent him to jail in disgrace, ending his brief, promising political career and shattering his life.

Sommers has lived on a large property in a small Vancouver Island community since shortly after he was paroled from jail in the early 1960s. He seldom before talked about the case. Sommers' dislike for the media remained firmly embedded, as much of what was written about him he considered untrue. There were "a whole lot of lies" in books published about his role in Social Credit's first B.C. government. He was still incensed about an assertion that he lost money playing cards in the Empress Hotel in Victoria. "I never played cards in the Empress in my life," he insisted.

Nearing 90, Sommers still wheeled his big old Chrysler around the neighbourhood, a "disabled" parking sticker on the car evidence of his advancing years. His memory, however, was sharp on the things he wanted to remember, if a little hesitant and hazy on some facts and forgetful of matters that he obviously shut out of his mind years ago, things he couldn't or didn't want to remember. His sardonic outlook and sense of humour prevailed, punctuated by flashes of temper and scathing comments about those he felt brought him down or stabbed him in the back. Sommers sprinkled his stories with reminiscences of his jail term, talking about "old cons" and the bumbling inefficiencies of the penal system as he knew it. He relished his accounts of one-upmanship wins over the penal bureaucracy and the "screws."

He talked as a survivor, a man who knew some of the worst things that life can deliver but still came back unbowed. He carved a new life out of the wreckage, proud that in the last quarter century he had been treated with respect in his working and private life. Seldom, very seldom, he said, were there any slurs about his being a former "con," convicted of conspiracy and bribery. Still hanging proudly in his home was a small, framed certificate given to those who sat as members of the legislature, thanking them for their services to the province.

Sommers insisted the money he took from Wick Gray was in the form of personal loans with no strings attached, and that he repaid all the money advanced to him. Referring to the much-cited carpets featured in the case, he asked who wouldn't pick up an offer to get goods wholesale. Part of his problem, he maintained, was that he never had much money, and he insisted that lawyers—"all the lawyers," and he dealt with several—assured him that the Crown had no case and he would never be convicted. Sommers quickly dismissed the report by Inspector Butler, saying there was nothing to it.

Sommers steadfastly maintained his innocence, damning his "enemies" and praising some of those he met during his mercurial political career. He was adamant that he was the victim of a plot, a ready target in a Liberal bid to try to bring down the neophyte Socred government, and he believed he still had "powerful enemies." Sommers had caustic comments about the lifestyle of sometime hard-drinking MLA Gordon Gibson, who first raised the "money talks" charges in the legislature. He dismissed *Vancouver Sun* and *Victoria Times* publishers Don Cromie and Stu Keate as nothing but "Liberal lackeys," their papers used as weapons to try to defeat the Socred government.

His remaining anger was directed primarily at those involved in prosecuting the case. He had harsh words for J.O. Wilson, who scathingly dismissed his libel suit against lawyer David Sturdy and later sentenced him to jail. He claimed that Wilson only became a judge because, like all the others appointed by Ottawa, he was approved by Bruce Hutchison. A renowned author and prominent B.C. editorialist with both the *Victoria Times* and the *Vancouver Sun*, the late Hutchison had powerful influence through his links with the federal Liberal government and the national Liberal party, according to Sommers. He labelled the judge "Mr. Gutless Wilson."

Sommers was sarcastic about the abilities of Stewart McMorran, the assistant prosecutor at his trial, who later became a judge. He said that one of the "back-stabbers" was his own lawyer, Angelo Branca, also later a judge. He alleged that at the last moment Branca told him he would make the Supreme Court of Canada appeal on only two points instead of the sixteen the lawyer had promised earlier.

His temporary disappearance into the U.S., and Waldo Skillings' role as a middleman with a financial offer from unidentified sources if he would stay out of B.C., were not events Sommers remembered well, though he maintained he didn't have to return to the province because the charges against him were not extraditable. Other details escaped him, except for the memory of meeting another man in trouble who had fled from B.C. When Sommers was in California, he encountered former Vancouver police chief Walter Mulligan, who at the time was working at Los Angeles airport. Mulligan had walked out on a royal commission hearing that ultimately found him to be the key participant in corruption that was rampant in the city's police department. Despite the findings, Mulligan was never charged and a number of years later quietly returned to live in Victoria.

Sommers first revealed that he was offered money to stay in the U.S. in a 1975 radio interview he gave to CKNW's Scott Dixon, although his disclosure did little to make the situation crystal clear.

In the Dixon interview, Sommers also emphasized that he had wanted to be tried alone. "I know what I did and I don't know what anyone else did." That was when he began to question the roles of the Gray brothers and Schultz, commenting, "I was beginning to feel maybe they did something."

"I got the big double-cross," Sommers told the radio reporter. He contended Skillings told him a deal had been made with the justice department so he would be charged alone. Sommers claimed he asked Skillings if he was speaking for Bennett or Bonner. He was told Bennett. He maintained that he was given the same assurance by both Bull and Skillings. Sommers said along with this assurance he was told exactly when the police would come to make the arrest and take him to Victoria police station. He even knew what the bail amount would be. Recalling the events today, Sommers got angry when he told how he found that instead of being charged alone, he was accused with the others and "there was an indictment a mile long." Instead of staying in Victoria as he expected, he was flown to Vancouver jail.

Sommers still had unkind words for his former cabinet colleague, Robert Bonner. Following the 1975 radio interview and stories by other reporters, Bonner denied Sommers' claim that the government had double-crossed him and dismissed the allegations and various contentions as a "lot of baloney." The former attorney general declined an invitation in 1999 to talk about the Sommers case, stating that it was all on the record.

Sommers remained convinced that he was double-crossed. His admiration for Premier Bennett, however, was still solid and untarnished, despite what Skillings allegedly told him about the premier's promise. He compared his old boss to H.R. MacMillan, whom he also liked, saying that in their presence one could feel their power and leadership, their vision, their confidence, and capability.

For the first time, Sommers publicly revealed that Premier Bennett offered to testify at his trial. Bennett would have stated that an FML was granted by cabinet decision and not solely by the forests minister. Strangely, said Sommers, this practice was not spelled out in writing in any government document, but it was the process at that time, and before the meeting with Taylor and McCutcheon, the cabinet discussed what it wanted from them. Sommers recalled, "There were about four cabinet ministers who attended the meeting in addition to Bennett, Bonner, and myself. Two of them were Ralph Chetwynd and Kenneth Kiernan. I don't remember the other two." Sommers said he declined Bennett's offer because he did not want to get the premier involved in the highly charged trial with all of its political ramifications.

Actually this was an astute move; in any close cross-examination, the premier's domination of the Empress Hotel meeting with E.P. Taylor, when the industrialist made his second bid for an FML, could have been disclosed. After Bennett heard Taylor's new pitch for a licence and extracted promises that he would invest in a mill and would build a forest road to the west coast of Vancouver Island, he agreed to the deal and told Sommers to sort out the details with the department. The jurors and the public could have learned clearly what was only suspected at the time about the premier's one-man rule, with the cabinet doing nothing but what it was told and rubber-stamping Bennett's on-the-spot decisions.

Sommers recalled that one Argus Corporation executive was unhappy with having to cough up the $750,000 for the road. Wally McCutcheon, "Taylor's hatchetman," angrily exploded when the demand was made, but he was quickly told by Taylor to sit down and be quiet. For E.P. it was a small cost of doing business when he was getting what he wanted. Sommers said he found Taylor to be "a gentleman, a very nice man," whom he met only twice.

Nona, Sommers' wife, a tiny, pleasant, friendly woman who stuck with her husband through all the troubles, smiled as she listened to him recount, with a mixture of humour and derision of authority, his life behind bars, the reminiscences of an "old con." While Sommers was in jail, she worked in a sawmill to support herself and her family. Their home was full of the usual photographs of family and friends, children and grandchildren. They also lived with the memories of a daughter who died much too young of leukemia.

Most of Sommers' sentence was served at William Head, a minimum security unit of the B.C. Penitentiary, frequently attacked by critics as a country-club-style establishment with a commanding view of sea and mountains on Vancouver Island near Victoria. He indicated he had little contact with Wick Gray either inside or outside, when both men were paroled at the same time. Sommers joked that he almost turned down parole because he didn't want to be beholden to anybody, saying he got free room and board, medical attention, and the chance to improve his education. The grimmer aspects of life behind bars, even minimum security, he didn't discuss. He wasn't intimidated by authority, stating that at times his conversation with the warden started "Well, Harry, what's your problem..."

Sommers applied to take mathematics courses by correspondence from Queen's University in Kingston, Ontario. He recalled working on papers while sitting on his cell bunk with the dangling legs of his cellmate in the upper bunk hanging in his face. When jail officials lost his papers and almost blew his chances of writing exams, Sommers, well aware of the power of the press, said he got action by threatening to tell the *Victoria Colonist* of his troubles.

He was critical of the so-called rehabilitation courses offered inmates in the 1950s. Some of the courses were impractical, said Sommers, asking, "Who wants to hire an ex-con as his bookkeeper?" He said he taught another inmate how to read, despite a rule that

While in jail, Sommers learned the art of piano tuning, a skill he made his living by after his release.

forbade inmates teaching anything to each other. Sommers admitted this rule was easily side-stepped, and it was what he learned in jail that reshaped his life. As a trumpet player and violinist, Sommers teamed up with another convict who was a piano virtuoso. From him he learned piano tuning, and this became his new vocation.

Sommers said he and his piano teacher proposed to the jail authorities that while serving their time they be allowed to retune and refinish pianos from local communities. They restrung the instruments and refinished the woodwork. He said their work was first class, even receiving the praise of a visiting Parole Board member from Montreal who was prominent in the arts. Eventually they involved other inmates in the work. Sommers said this training was practical and something ex-prisoners could turn their hands to when they got out. When released, Sommers started his own piano tuning business. At one point he had two employees, and he got contracts from school boards, Canadian Legions, and other groups and associations on Vancouver Island. He was proud of his work, noting that a prominent international pianist, who visited the area and performed on a piano Sommers had tuned, said it produced a tone that was near perfection for the concert instrument and equal to anything the artist had heard elsewhere. Sommers proudly repeated that he was well received by all he worked for and was given their respect, his past ignored.

Asked for his opinion of the sorry state of B.C.'s forest industry and its continuing crisis, he said he had no new ideas, though better reforestation and management were obvious measures. He took no satisfaction in the fact that his predictions of almost 50 years earlier, that overcutting in the Vancouver Forest District would lead to its partial destruction, loss of jobs, and the death of some coastal lumbering communities, had come to pass. Sommers believed that the policies, or lack of them, in successive provincial governments, along with the intransigence of labour and industry, had contributed to today's debacle.

Bob Sommers hadn't seen many of his old political cronies in the last 25 years, and he didn't care. His downfall was a long time ago, his life had taken a different course, and in a mellowing old age he kept the memories he treasured. When telling the stories of his heyday and demise, his temper sometimes flared, but quickly died, as he raked his old foes over the coals for what he claimed they did to him. He obviously was sustained, and had been throughout his third career, by a fierce conviction that he was innocent of the crimes that sent

Victoria photographer Jim Ryan visited Bob Sommers shortly after his release from William Head Jail. Sommers' family—including wife Nona on left and his daughter—stood by him throughout the ordeal. After her husband's conviction, Nona Sommers told reporters she didn't want him to go into politics in the first place.

him to jail and created the Socreds' first and biggest crisis and scandal. In Sommers' mind he was always "Honest Bob," doing his job for the people and his party.

Was Justice Done?

The verdicts in this celebrated case left the public confused and confounded. Many could not understand why only Sommers and Wick Gray were convicted while Charlie Schultz, BCFP, and John Gray escaped. To this day, questions remain unanswered.

In his summation, Judge Wilson stressed to the jury that Charles Eversfield, Wick Gray's former accountant, and Trevor Daniels, BCFP's former top financial executive, were the key prosecution witnesses in the case. He also found, however, that Eversfield was a co-conspirator, the one who helped initially to cover up the transactions. Wilson also reminded the jury of the defence argument that Daniels bore a grudge because he was passed over for the BCFP presidency.

The jurors had listened attentively to the evidence of Eversfield and watched his performance in the witness box under the heaviest fire the defence lawyers could muster. He was accused of trying to blackmail Gray for money, and there was at least one attempt to link him to the alleged Gibson-Sturdy Liberal plot to bring down Sommers and the Socreds. Eversfield denied it all, not wavering in his testimony and not being caught out in any apparent lie or error. He was backed up by the mountain of documents presented by the prosecution, so numerous and so involved that Judge Wilson and the jury had difficulty sorting through them, never mind understanding them all.

The trial also heard the significant evidence of Trevor Daniels, the BCFP executive who, because of his position, obviously knew the details of the company's financial dealings. E.P. Taylor had thought enough of his abilities to send him from Toronto to join the Vancouver firm. Daniels told an unwavering story about his discussions with BCFP president Hector Munro. He had voiced objections and explained his fears about the implications regarding bribery that could arise from the financial dealings with Schultz and Gray in pursuit of FML #22. The defence tried to portray Daniels as a man whose ambition had been thwarted and who held a grudge, but his actions did not indicate this.

In today's world, the unfortunate demise of a company president involved in a growing political scandal would be seized on by the media as a major development in a continuing story. His sudden death a few hours after intensive questioning by the police would be carefully dissected, and conclusions would be drawn. Hector Munro was a badly shaken man when he left his office and went home. He knew that the police had evidence linking BCFP to the allegations that there had been attempts to bribe Sommers in an effort to obtain an FML. He knew that he faced sweeping public scrutiny of his performance, both within the company and in his private life. He faced public humiliation and the possibility of going to jail. More than anyone else, he knew what the company had done and he knew Trevor Daniels was prepared to talk. Munro's whole life had been based on his established reputation and the prestige of his position. With all of this in jeopardy, he could no longer face his friends or his family.

Hector Munro, a virile, active, healthy man, died that night. The papers reported only that Munro died suddenly; there was no tie-in to the unfolding Sommers affair. Why the media did not investigate cannot be explained and did them no credit. Since the "money talks" allegations, they had poked and pried into many corners, questioned many people, chased rumours and angles, but for reasons of their own, they did not pursue this critical development. In the 1950s, even more than today, it would have been classed by many as a cruel encroachment on the privacy of a bereaved family, but this has always been one of the unpleasant aspects for a reporter getting at the facts and the truth.

Munro's mentor, H.R. MacMillan, made it clear years later in his biography that he never doubted Munro took his own life. The old timber baron had been fond of Munro and had confidence in his skills and business acumen. His contention was never refuted. In his book on the W.A.C. Bennett years, David Mitchell reiterates that Munro committed suicide. In that fateful December when Munro became the greatest casualty of the Sommers affair, there were many who drew their own conclusions that he had killed himself. The jurors at the Sommers trial became conversant with all aspects of the affair during the months they sat and listened to the evidence and the plots unfold. It is difficult to believe that at least some of them did not link Munro's suspicious death to the charges against BCFP as another factor in their final decision.

Another disturbing question that remains unanswered concerns Wick Gray's financial situation. If Gray's company PCS was on the verge of liquidation in 1954, he would not have had money to loan Sommers. As time went by, large deposits appeared in some of Gray's accounts. These were listed on Schultz's accounts as payments to Gray for public relations work. This was at a time when a well-paid public relations consultant brought home no more than $400 per month, so Schultz's payments to Gray were extremely generous if they enabled Gray to loan Sommers $7,000. If, as the evidence suggests, Schultz provided the money Gray loaned to Sommers, how could Gray alone be guilty of giving bribes?

Throughout the case there was always the overriding suggestion that money talked, and perhaps it whispered when it came time for the verdicts as well. BCFP was owned by Argus and one of Canada's richest men, E.P. Taylor. The company was found not guilty. C.D. Schultz was part of the Vancouver establishment, the son of a judge, himself trained as a lawyer. The jury could not agree on a guilty verdict for him. Only Gray and Sommers were found guilty, despite the fact that to the end, Robert Bonner maintained there was not enough corroborated evidence to convict Sommers. He said the former minister would not have been convicted if he had not taken the stand. Was Sommers' halting testimony what most convinced jurors of his and Gray's guilt?

The jurors were out a long time before reaching their verdicts, but it had been a lengthy and complicated case. Under Canadian law, the panel was forbidden to tell which of the issues divided them for so long before their decision was reached. Their conclusions remain puzzling, however, even more than 40 years later. They were undecided on as many issues as they resolved.

Since the Sommers case made front-page headlines, many more B.C. politicians have been forced to resign as a result of misconduct or misdeeds. One of the more recent scandals occurred in the spring of 1999, when Premier Glen Clark's home was raided by police. It was then revealed that the NDP leader was under investigation for allegedly helping a neighbour who had applied for a casino licence in exchange for renovations on his home and summer cottage. Clark denied that he had influenced the licensing process in any way, but the release of a search warrant raised more questions and suggested he was guilty of a monumental lapse of judgment if nothing else. No charges had been laid against Clark when he resigned as premier.

Clark was the third B.C. premier in ten years to step down before his term was finished. His immediate predecessors, Bill Vander Zalm, a Socred, and Mike Harcourt of the NDP, resigned earlier in the midst of rumours, scandal, and charges of conflict of interest. It was the nefarious Dave Stupich who forced the resignation of Harcourt, who did not speak out against his former colleague, a party fundraiser, Nanaimo MLA and finance minister for Dave Barretts' NDP government, until after Stupich had pleaded guilty to fraud in the summer of 1999. Stupich's accounting practices as collector and distributor of funds from charity bingo games through the Nanaimo Commonwealth Holding Society made the NDP rich, along with Stupich and his family. He was reported to have diverted more than a million dollars that was to have gone to charity. In the end, because prosecution was delayed for so long, Stupich escaped the consequences of his actions by reason of old age and mental incapacity. Circumstances gave him a much lighter sentence than Sommers had served, although he pleaded guilty to a more serious crime.

Because politicians have considerable power, they try too often to use it to better the fortunes of the party they represent or, on occasion, to line their own pockets or those of their friends. They use the tried and seemingly acceptable, but nonetheless publicly unacceptable, vehicles of patronage and party favouritism. Forced into defensive positions that reflect badly on their own public image, and on their party and politicians in general, they tend to hang on too long before stepping aside. And each time this occurs, be it at the provincial or federal level, each time there is a constituency payoff, a patronage appointment, favouritism, or partisanship, the public loses a little more confidence in and respect for the politicians who hold the future of the province or the country in their hands.

When Premier W.A.C. Bennett came to power in 1952, he swore that payoffs and patronage had destroyed the Coalition government and vowed his honest little group would never stoop so low. He tried, but somehow politics got the better of him.

B.C. now has a conflict-of-interest commissioner, and in view of recent developments, many wonder if the terms of reference should be broadened to create something like an ethics commissioner, who, after much initial consultation, would have the authority to set standards and discipline politicians and bureaucrats who stepped out of bounds. Ethics is now a recognized course at many universities; it's time to move beyond the theoretical and the classroom and into the realm of the real world.

Politicians entering the fray are always in search of power to effect change, but a little altruism is also essential if the calibre and image of those in charge of the country are to improve. Maybe then resignations will be rare and politicians will regain the respect of voters.

EPILOGUE

The Immortal Forests

Did the Sommers case affect forest policy in B.C.? What were the ramifications of decisions made during the early 1950s when the minister of lands and forests accepted loans from his friends in the business? Nearly 50 years later, the answer to the first question is no, and the answer to the second, none.

Ray Williston succeeded Sommers as forests minister and held the position from 1956 until 1972. He perhaps did more than any other politician to improve utilization and encourage development of B.C.'s Interior forests. With the very large and productive Vancouver Forest District fully allocated, he concentrated his efforts on the expansion of the Interior industry, including that in the Prince George region, which was his home.

Williston found his first deputy minister, Dr. C.D. Orchard, dogmatic and unable to deal with some of the difficult decisions that needed to be made. This was the man who first turned down the BCFP application for an FML and so indirectly precipitated the Sommers case. Fortunately, Orchard retired soon after Williston became minister, and the man from Prince George was able to successfully revamp the forest service. During his term the Forest Service identified six forest regions in the province. Today they are known as the Vancouver, Prince Rupert, Prince George, Cariboo, Kamloops, and Nelson Forest Districts.

For six years in the legislature, Williston contended with the combative Gordon Gibson, who ran successfully in North Vancouver in 1960. Gibson continued his campaign for the small logger both in and out of the House. In 1961 he told a convention of truckloggers that in the forest industry, "money is still talking today." By then Gibson maintained that Sommers was "no more guilty than dozens of others." He was unrelenting in his pursuit until he finally retired from politics in 1966, turning his interests to the creation of a tourist resort, Maui Lu, in Hawaii. The colourful Gibson died in 1986.

Forest policy during the twentieth century has been plagued by poor performance on the part of nearly everyone involved, probably least of all by Robert Sommers. It was the companies that obtained licences to cut trees, and the politicians with conflicting agendas and short-term objectives, that have impacted B.C.'s forests most severely and continue to do so. What was first feared in 1912 is now coming to pass, and B.C. in the late 1990s is running out of profitable, harvestable timber.

Among the hundreds of pages of factual but dull prose and necessary statistics in the Sloan Report is a small passage that tellingly reveals the soul of a man who loved his province, its forests, and the sweeping outdoors in which he spent his leisure time. To Judge Sloan, a Nanaimo-born British Columbian and quietly proud of it, the preservation of the forests in a managed and caring way was a precious cause. People eventually would consume the world's oil and gas and its minerals, but the forests were immortal. They would always grow again. In a few lyric paragraphs he expressed his wish that more young men—forestry 40 years ago didn't employ many women—would pursue it as a career, not only for the financial rewards, but for its wonderful opportunities. It is not often that a royal commissioner turns eloquent or emotional about an industrial inquiry, but Judge Sloan did. He wrote:

> The green and shadowed world of the forest and the tranquillity of its cathedral silences is an unknown world to most.
>
> Forestry is for men who can suffer its harsher moments, strengthened by an inner conviction that they are blazing trails, leading forever into the beckoning future.
>
> They are working with a great, elemental living force.
>
> They are the pioneers of a last frontier and if they work well, future generations in the long years ahead will gratefully remember them.
>
> The abundant, healthy and magnificent forests of the future will stand as a living monument to their dedication to this ideal.
>
> In time the earth will be sucked dry of its oil and filched of its minerals, but the managed and protected forests, forever renewing themselves, are immortal.

Those who have ventured into the trackless vastness of our coast forest and travelled its unknown ways, and those who, in the Interior, have climbed and stood upon the crest of a lonely hill, thrusting abruptly from a limitless sea of green that sweeps in all directions, expanding until it darkens and loses its identity at the far reaches of an encircling horizon, will understand the spirit of the things whereof I speak.

The second Sloan Royal Commission, perhaps more than the first, set the stage for forest policy through the remainder of the century, and Gordon Sloan's untimely death left the process in limbo. Throughout the years since then, the flaws have become more pronounced, hindsight providing the vision that was not possible earlier. With no secure long-term tenure, forest companies, knowing they were subject to the whims of whatever government was in power, planted new forests as required, but they did not cultivate and improve them. As long as the tax money poured in from the forest companies, governments failed to spend the necessary funds to encourage better harvesting methods and improvements to the more valuable species. As a result, trees from the U.S. and Sweden are now considered superior to the once mighty forests of B.C. They are certainly cheaper to harvest. According to F.L.C. Reed, forest consultant and University of B.C. professor, it is not too late to bring the mighty forests back—there is about ten years to do it—but for the present their quality has deteriorated, and much more must be spent on enhancement of the valuable species which grow best in B.C.

In addition to political interference at national and international levels, which resulted in countervailing duties and restrictive taxes for largely political reasons, the forest industry in recent times has been under attack from many directions. Everyone seems to want a piece of the B.C. landscape: environmental conservationists are trying to conserve old-growth forests; outdoor recreationists want more parkland; ecologists want to isolate ecosystems so they can be studied; fisheries managers want more streambank protection; and Native peoples want to settle aboriginal land claims by taking large blocks of forest land for themselves. It is remarkable that any of the forests survive for the use of the forest industry, but they do. The government, in its attempt to address the objectives of all the people, has developed such a complicated structure that Patrick Nagle wrote recently in the *Vancouver Sun*, "The system has become so cumbersome and expensive that investing in output costs more than can be recovered." Change is required and it can no longer be postponed.

It seems that attitudes have changed little since B.C.'s first chief forester, H.R. MacMillan, left the civil service in 1919 because the government of the day was not providing the funds to do the job properly. H.R. built his own empire and probably contributed more to the industry than any other visionary of the twentieth century. During the second Sloan Commission he became concerned for the small logger and made a number of suggestions to assist with the survival of this sector. This was also the issue that brought Gordon Gibson into the legislature.

In the book *H.R.: A Biography of H.R. MacMillan*, Ken Drushka states in the concluding paragraphs:

> It has been forty years since MacMillan stood before Chief Justice Gordon Sloan and predicted what would happen if forest policies built around the Forest Management Licence system were implemented. To the great detriment of the people of B.C., he turned out to be right. By 1975, when Peter Pearse, the first recipient of the MacMillan prize in forestry, conducted another royal commission on forestry, many of MacMillan's predictions had come true. The extent of corporate concentration had become, as Pearse stated, a matter of "urgent public concern." Pearse also warned that existing policies were leading to future timber shortages, which could result in mills being closed and workers losing their jobs.
>
> By the early 1990s, MacMillan's predictions and Pearse's added warnings—both of them ignored by successive governments—could no longer be disregarded. As MacMillan and his colleagues had anticipated, under a tenure system characterized by public ownership of the land, no adequate forest management capability could develop. Private investment in publicly owned forests had not occurred and successive governments had spent their forest revenues elsewhere. Although new forests had been started on logged-off lands, they were producing nowhere near their potential volumes or values. Annual timber harvests had to be drastically reduced, mills were closed, workers laid off, and communities faced economic hardship, if not outright dissolution.
>
> In the face of these economic and social calamities, MacMillan's vision for B.C. of a diversified economy based on stewardship of the province's renewable natural resources continues to be relevant. His alternative to the system which has prevailed, and failed, for the past 40 years is still a valid choice. MacMillan's ideas—the potential he saw in British Columbia, the policies he proposed, and the society he envisaged—may well turn out to be his most enduring legacy.

The corporate takeovers predicted by H.R. MacMillan in his 50,000-word brief to the Sloan Commission have also occurred. BCFP, the company at the centre of the Sommers case, changed ownership a number of times during its 40-year history. It ceased to exist in 1988 when it was purchased, along with Crown Forest Products, by New Zealand's Fletcher Challenge. The two former companies became Fletcher Challenge Canada. Since then the shape and scope of Fletcher Challenge has also changed and expanded. Ever larger companies continue to gobble each other up, and in 1999 even MacMillan Bloedel was threatened with extinction as U.S. forest giant Weyerhaeuser, one of the largest forest companies in the world, offered to purchase all its shares.

New methods, new products, new markets, new owners—a restructuring process is underway in the forests of B.C. on many fronts. It is a process the likes of which has not been seen before on the West Coast. If it is successful, everyone wins. If it is not, everyone will lose.

The impact of the Sommers case was hardly felt in the forests of the province, only on the lives of those involved. Some 50 years later, the forests are about to affect the lives of many more people than ever before.

APPENDIX I

Election Records

Bob Sommers won three times at the polls in his political career, which began in the spring of 1952 and ended when he automatically lost his seat on conviction in late 1958.

The official Elections B.C. records show the details of his support.

1952 Election (Multiple choice system)

First Count:

Johnson, Ering Olaf (CCF)	2,541	22.02%
Sommers, Robert Edward (BCSCL)	3,979	34.48%
Turnbull, Alexander Douglas (Lib)	3,331	28.86%
Wright, Charles Alfred Holstead (PC)	1,690	14.64%

Final Count

Sommers	5,917	55.20%
Turnbull	4,803	44.80

1953 Election (Multiple choice system)

First Count

Fletcher, Emil George (PC)	621	5.56%
Muirhead, Samuel Clayton (CCF)	3,470	31.06%
Sommers, Robert Edward (SC)	4,182	37.43%
Wetmore, Douglas T. (Lib)	2,899	25.95%

Final Count

Muirhead	4,549	44.05%
Sommers	5,778	55.95%

1956 Election (Single vote system)

McRae, Thomas Alexander (PC)	252	2.48%
Muirhead, Samuel Clayton (CCF)	2,839	27.98%
Sommers, Robert Edward (SC)	5,097	50.23%
Waldie, William Thompson (Lib)	1,960	19.31%

(In the by-election on December 15, 1958, to replace Sommers, Social Credit candidate Donald Brothers got 3,170 votes, 30.07%—a very narrow victory won on a closely split vote. The CCF got 26.63%, the Liberal 22.43%, and the Tory 20.87%)

Elections B.C. records also reveal support for W.A.C. Bennett's Socreds during the Sommers years.

Election 1952 (Multiple choice system)

Final Count

Christian Democratic Party	1,318	0.20%	
CCF	231,756	34.30%	18 seats
Independent	0		
Labour (Party)	1,758	0.26%	1 seat
Labour Progressive Party	931	0.14%	
Labour Representation Cte.	0		
Liberal Party	170,674	25.26%	6 seats
Progressive Conservative Party	65,285	9.66%	4 seats
Social Credit (BCSCL)	203,932	30.18%	19 seats
Socialist Party of Canada	0		

In the final count there were 675,654 votes cast, 212 candidates competing for 48 seats.

Election 1953 (Multiple choice system)

Final Count

Christian Democratic Party	752	.12%	
CCF	194,414	29.48%	14 seats
Independent	0		
Labour (Party)	1,793	.27%	1 seat
Labour Progressive Party	816	.12%	

Liberal Party	154,090	23.36%	4 seats
Progressive Conservative Party	7,326	1.11%	1 seat
Social Credit (Party)	300,372	45.54%	28 seats

In the final count there were 659,563 votes cast, 229 candidates competing for 48 seats.

1956 Election (Single vote system)

CCF	231,511	28.32%	10 seats
Independent and other	3,178	0.39%	
Labour (Party)	1,321	0.16%	1 seat
Labour Progressive Party	3,381	0.41%	
Liberal Party	177,922	21.77%	2 seats
Progressive Conservative Party	25,373	3.11%	
Social Credit (Party)	374,711	45.84%	39 seats

There were 817,397 votes cast, 199 candidates competing for 52 seats.

APPENDIX 2

The Fall of Social Credit

The reign of Bennett the First ended in 1972 when B.C.'s first socialist government came to power under colourful if erratic David Barrett, a former social worker turned politician. A split vote this time put the New Democratic Party into power. Twenty years earlier, Harold Winch had twice suffered the opposite result. The NDP took 40 percent of the vote and elected 38 members, whereas Social Credit got 31 percent but only elected 10 members, including Bennett. The Liberals had five members and the Tories two.

Barrett had a short but tumultuous reign, punctuated by opposition from the province's mining and forest industries and, surprisingly, also problems with the labour movement.

Bennett remained as opposition leader until his retirement in June 1973. At a leadership convention in the fall, Bennett saw his son Bill, aged 41, as his successor, although the younger Bennett had never before run for elected office. Bill Bennett ran for his father's seat in the South Okanagan, but refused his father's overt campaign assistance in order to defuse NDP accusations that he was simply "daddy's little boy." He won the seat. Among the losers was Conservative Darril Warren, who shortly afterward resigned as party leader.

Bennett senior played a significant behind-the-scenes role in mustering party support to elect his son at the leadership convention in November. The younger Bennett won easily on the first ballot. Significant for Bill Bennett's career was the election of Grace McCarthy as party president. Along with W.A.C., she tirelessly travelled the province, drumming up Socred support for the next election, and by the mid-1970s Social Credit had become the largest provincial political party in Canadian history.

Barrett's NDP government quickly became unpopular and was dubbed the "Chile of the North" (a reference to Salvador Allende's socialist government) because of its sweeping social reforms. Heavy mining industry royalties and increased industry taxation, along with a land reserve act that had farmers complaining they were serfs on their own property, were moves that contributed to an outflow of capital from the province and a halt to many development projects. Under the pressure, the mercurial Barrett called a surprise election in 1975 after only three years in office. Bill Bennett won easily on December 11, taking 50 percent of the vote and routing the NDP. The final count was Socreds, 35 members; New Democrats, 18; and one each for the Liberals and Conservatives.

The younger Bennett was the second son of W.A.C. He grew up in Kelowna in a well-disciplined household, run by his mother because of the frequent absences of his father. He was one of three children. He had an older brother, Russell James, and a sister, Mary Anita. Like his brother, Bill bypassed university to enter the family business. He did not show any political ambitions until 1973.

Bennett the Younger was the premier for eleven years. He never quite shook the shadow of his father, and the opposition along with the media dubbed him "Mini-WAC." He lacked verve and style, and his reserved personality kept him from inciting the heights of adulation experienced by his father. He had a button-down, bottom-line approach to government.

By 1986 his government was beset with problems, and many of his supporters believed that after wins in 1979 and 1983, he was unlikely to take another election. The province was in an economic slump, the premier's style had made him many enemies, and at age 53 he decided to retire.

Five years later he became embroiled in an insider trading case that involved his brother and Herb Doman, chairman and chief executive officer of Doman Industries Ltd. Bennett the Younger is now serving a ten-year securities trading ban imposed by the B.C. Securities Commission. Russell Bennett and Doman fought the securities trading ban all the way to the Supreme Court of Canada and lost. They also face a ban on serving as officers or directors of a company, a move that may leave Doman unable to manage his own firm. In addition, the Securities Commission has suggested they may have to contribute a million dollars to help pay the costs of the lengthy hearings they have instituted over the past eleven years.

The Socred leadership race in 1986 went to William Vander Zalm, an ebullient, eccentric businessman dubbed "Willy Wooden Shoes" by acerbic *Sun* columnist Alan Fotheringham. Vander Zalm garnered many headlines before revelations of improper real estate deals forced him from office in 1991. The Socreds were thrown into total confusion, and in a quickly called leadership convention, cabinet minister Rita Johnston, 55, won 51 percent of the vote to become party leader and therefore premier. In an election only seven months later, the Socreds were annihilated. Mrs. Johnston lost her seat to Penny Priddy, who became minister of health in the NDP government of Mike Harcourt.

Some 30 years after they burst onto the B.C. scene, the Socreds were through. For the rest of the decade they had only a handful of members in the House, none at all as the century ran out. Even Vander Zalm pulled the plug on the party when he decided in 1998 to have another crack at politics, winning the presidency of the small, right-wing B.C. Reform Party.

BIBLIOGRAPHY

Primary sources

National Library, Ottawa
National Archives, Ottawa
B.C. Archives, Victoria
City of Vancouver Archives
Vancouver Public Library, Special Collections
North Vancouver Public Library
B.C. Ministry of Forests

Books

Drushka, Ken. *H.R.: A Biography of H.R. MacMillan*. Madeira Park, BC: Harbour Publishing, 1995.

Gibson, Gordon. *Bull of the Woods*. Vancouver: Douglas and MacIntyre, 1980.

Keene, Roger and David C. Humphreys. *Conversations with W.A.C. Bennett*. Toronto: Methuen Publications, 1980.

Mitchell, David. *W.A.C.: Bennett and the Rise of British Columbia*. Vancouver: Douglas and McIntyre, 1983.

Shelford, Cyril. *From Snowshoes to Politics*. Victoria: Orca Book Publishers, 1987.

Sherman, Paddy. *Bennett*. Toronto: McClelland and Stewart, 1966.

Williston, Eileen and Betty Keller. *Forests, Power and Policy: The Legacy of Ray Williston*. Prince George, BC: Caitlin Press, 1997.

Newspapers

Trail Times
Vancouver News Herald
Vancouver Province
Vancouver Sun
Victoria Colonist
Victoria Times

ACKNOWLEDGEMENTS

Special thanks to the following for their comments and assistance:
Robert E. Sommers, former MLA, cabinet minister, and musician
Deane Finlayson, Nanaimo realtor, former B.C. Conservative Party
     leader and provincial candidate
Cyril Shelford, former Socred MLA and cabinet minister
Gordon Gibson Jr., political writer
Fred Moonen, Forest Industry Government Affairs
Len Marquis, Toronto writer, musician, film producer
F.L.C. Reed, UBC forestry professor and forest industry consultant
Jennie Miller, Elections B.C.
Chubba Hashu, Forest Industrial Relations
Elizabeth Steele, Forest Alliance of B.C.
Frank Walden, former reporter and public relations consultant
Vera Lucas and Sheena Macdonald, research

PHOTO CREDITS

BCARS: Front cover (I-29413) (I-60025) (I-60027) (NA-13779),back cover (I-29407), p. 3 (I-29407), p. 6 (NA-13779), p. 13 (F-08357), p. 16 (I-60025), p. 18 (l: D-09131, r: B-07943), p. 23 (I-60028), p. 25 (I-60027), p. 26 (I-32475), p. 28 (B-06613), p. 31 (G-02440), p. 33 (F-08614), p. 35 (I-32575), p. 47 (I-60032), p. 48 (H-06827), p. 50 (H-01533), p. 55 (NA-10137), p. 57 (p. NA-27043), p. 62 (G-03923), p. 62 (l: I-32501, r: C-07953), p. 66 (NA-22319), p. 73 (I-32556), p. 74 (I-50041), p. 81 (NA-22402), p. 82/83 (G-00835), p. 85 (I-25994), p. 88 (I-32597), p. 94 (I-26104), p. 96 (F-08358), p. 101 (t: H-01741), p. 108 (I-60026), p. 121 (I-01125), p. 126 (I-32587), p. 152 (I-32424), p. 168 (I-60029), p. 170 (I-60031). **B.C. Hydro Information Services**: p. 101, b. Chris Gaynor: p. 41, (#6). Peter Johnson: p. 162. **North Vancouver Museum & Archives:** p. 119 (#6702). **Vancouver Public Library**: p. 8 (#63869), p. 37 (#78848-B), p. 45, p. 87 (#45231), p. 115 (#63635), p. 143. *Vancouver Sun*: p. 149, p. 128.

     The photos on pages 16, 23, 25, 47, 62, 108, 168, 170 are from the Jim Ryan Collection at the BC. Archives and Records Service.

     The photo on the back cover represents the classic ritual of felling the spar tree in the B.C. forest industry in the 1950s.

INDEX

Betty O'Keefe was a reporter on the *Vancouver Province* for seven years in the mid-1950s and then worked in corporate communications for fifteen years. Later she was commissioned to write two corporate biographies— *Brenda: The Story of a Mine* and *The Mines of Babine Lake*.

Ian Macdonald has worked on the *Victoria Colonist*, the *Vancouver Province,* and the *Vancouver Sun*. He was legislative reporter for the *Sun* in Victoria for five years and bureau chief in Ottawa from 1965 to 1970. He worked in media relations for the prime minister's office, and was head of Transport Canada Information. He has written for magazines, radio, television, and film.

Since 1994 Macdonald and O'Keefe have applied themselves to writing projects related to West Coast history and contemporary issues (*The Klondike's 'Dear Little Nugget'* and *Earthquake: Your Chances, Your Options, Your Future*). *The Mulligan Affair: Top Cop on the Take,* their first book published by Heritage House in 1997, was nominated for the City of Vancouver Book Award. *The Final Voyage of the Princess Sophia* followed in 1998 and, with *The Sommers Scandal* now between covers, Betty and Ian have begun research for a new book based on true crime and a clash between the White and Chinese communities of Vancouver in the 1920s.